The Holy Bible

The Holy Bible

No Free Will

Nick Vale

Copyright © 2023 by Nick Vale.

All rights reserved. No part of this publication may be reproduced, distributed, or transmitted in any form or by any means, including photocopying, recording, or other electronic or mechanical methods, without the prior written permission of the publisher, except in the case of brief quotations embodied in critical reviews and certain other noncommercial uses permitted by copyright law. For permission requests, write to the publisher, addressed "Attention: Permissions Coordinator," at the address below.

Nick Vale/Author's Tranquility Press
2706 Station Club Drive SW
Marietta, GA 30060
www.authorstranquilitypress.com

Ordering Information:
Quantity sales. Special discounts are available on quantity purchases by corporations, associations, and others. For details, contact the "Special Sales Department" at the address above.

The Holy Bible: No Free Will/Nick Vale
Paperback:978-1-957208-99-2
Ebook:978-1-957546-00-1

CONTENTS

Foreword - Part One 9
   In The Beginning 9
Foreword - Part Two 13
   In The Beginning 13

Book One by The Steward 15
   Definition 15
Book Two by The Introducer 19
   Introduction 19
Book Three by Nick Vale 23
   Understanding 23
Book Four by Nick Vale 30
   The Word "Free" Confuses 30
Book Five by Nick Vale 37
   The Illusion of Free Will 37
Book Six by The Absorber 41
   How It All Works 41
Book Seven by The Causer 47
   Law Of Causation 47
Book Eight by The Conditioner 55
   Everything Conditions You 55
Book Nine by The Conduit 60
   Paradigm Shift 60

- Book Ten by The Custodian 62
  - Myth Of Free Will 62
- Book Eleven by The Gifter 82
  - The Greatest Gift 82
- Book Twelve by The Reality Teller 87
  - It Is What It Is 87
- Book Thirteen by The Reflector 92
  - Reflections 92
- Book Fourteen by The Reporter 97
  - Man Does Not Have Free Will 97
- Book Fifteen by The Reviewer 104
  - Review 104
- Book Sixteen by The Simplifier 110
  - 150 Quotes 110
- Book Seventeen by The Unconscious 126
  - The Unconscious 126
- Book Eighteen by The Vindicator 134
  - Vindication 134
- Book Nineteen by The Harmer 143
  - Why Free Will is Bad for Society 143
- Book Twenty by Occam's razor 147
  - The Law of Parsimony 147
- Book Twenty One: by Nick Vale 149
  - Epilogue 149
- Book Twenty Two 157
  - About the author, Contact the author, Dedication, Many Thanks 157
- Book Twenty-Three by Quick Summary 161
  - Why Free Will Is Impossible 161

New truth is often uncomfortable.

This is especially true for the holders of power the new truth threatens.

New truth is often looked at as blasphemy.

Amen,

www.nofreewill.info

www.nofreewill.org

"Rather than love, than money, than fame, give me truth."

— Henry David Thoreau

Foreword - Part One

In The Beginning . . .

- The #1 reason why people believe in free will is because they want it to be true. Wanting something to be true does not make it true.
- As of the publication date of this Holy Bible, the vast majority of people on planet earth do in fact believe in free will. People believe in free will because conformity and feeling "normal" is a form of pleasure.
- People have no choice but to always go towards pleasure and away from pain. People who believe in the nonsense of free will reflect this psychological law.
- When "do this—to get that" no longer works you will need a belief system to accommodate that reality.
- People are always doing the very best they can at the time.
- Law and Order will not break down with the advent of the knowledge contained in this book. Actions will always still have consequences.
- We were taught that man's will is free. We were taught all wrong.
- We could not have done otherwise with who we were at the time, the knowledge we had at the time, and the way the entire state of the universe was at the time.

Once you fully internalize that there is no such thing as "free will" will you then understand that all of life is pre-determined. You simply have no choice but to always be doing the very best you can AT THE TIME with the knowledge you had at the time. **You do not get to choose how intelligent you are, were, or will become.**

You must become "ready" for everything (including reading this new kind of Bible). Physical, emotional, mental, and psychological states all have a causal history to them (cause and effect). You cannot control when you become ready for things. You cannot control when you change your mind, beliefs, or perspective about something. Once again, you did not choose how intelligent you are.

You are not a failure if you fail at something because you do not have free will.

If you could have done otherwise, rest assured, you would have done otherwise.

"Trading Places Theory" also refutes free will:
How can there be "ultimate moral responsibility?"

Trading Places Theory: Say this to yourself . . .

"If I were an 'evil' other person, I'd be that 'evil' other person. Atom for Atom, Quark for Quark, Neuron for Neuron, Neutrino for Neutrino, Boson for Boson, and the same exact 'evil' mind and soul and all . . . I'd have that person's same exact consciousness.

With his/her exact same genetics, his/her exact same conditioning (how he/she was raised), and his/her exact same 'evil' mind and soul. I'd be him/her in every exact and conceivable way and would've acted the same exact way in every regard possible. 'Free Will' is nowhere to be found."

Q: Why do people continue to believe in "free will?"

A: They have an emotional/psychological attachment to it. They feel better believing in it than not believing in it. The opposite is also true—these people become psychologically and emotionally disturbed or unhinged by not believing in it ("free will"). Simply put, not believing in free will greatly depresses them. People have no choice but to believe in free will because to do otherwise would inflict severe psychological and emotional damage upon themselves and in effect would shatter their entire life paradigm (world view). Amen.

- Everything is conditioning. You have no choice but to always go towards pleasure and away from pain. You also have no choice but to always be doing the very best you can at the time. Amen.
- Free Will is a very harmful belief. It makes people believe they are failures when they cannot succeed at something. Amen.
- We are not free to choose things that do not occur to us at the time. Amen.
- Society will soon have to learn something called "pragmatic blameless responsibility" or just simply put "blameless or faultless responsibility." Amen.
- Man can self-cause nothing. Not even a single thought. Amen.
- Yes you are pragmatically responsible for your karma (cause and effect). But ultimately and fundamentally you are not responsible for your karma (cause and effect)." Amen.
- Human beings are an overly pragmatic species. Believing in free will is simply the most pragmatic way of being in this world. This is one of the reasons why human beings incorrectly believe in the magical quality of "free will." Amen.
- Human beings are really human computers. The two most important programs or operating systems that we are running are the pleasure principle and the optimization imperative (always doing the very best we can at the time). In a nutshell, this means we always have no choice but to do what we do and we could not have done otherwise (with the knowledge we had at the time). Amen.
- When an accident or mistake occurs and you did everything in your power to avoid it, then it must be called fate. There is no other choice in the matter. Amen.
- The last great truth to be discovered is that free will is false and is a grand illusion. We are just a witness to our own life. Amen.

Dear Reader,

Since most people have been conditioned to believe in free will, changing the world's point of view will be extremely hard. Our educational and mental health system need to be changed as soon as possible with regard to this free will issue. I believe that deep down people always prefer the truth over lies and this leaves a window of hope. If people can become intrigued they'll investigate, try to find the truth, and eventually come to the inevitable conclusion that free will is a lie. Please join me in this effort.

- Change is a causal process. Just because human beings don't have free wills doesn't mean they cannot change. As soon as human beings internalize that there is more pleasure in not believing in free will than there is in believing in it, will they be ready for this change. In fact change is what living in the universe is all about.

People are constantly changing based on the stimuli they encounter in their lives. You can help someone change by clearly explaining to them the teachings of this new kind of Bible (you become the new stimuli they encounter).

- Change = (Cause and Effect) x Time

One moment in time creates the next moment in time. Look at the back cover and just picture each domino as a moment in time. Each domino falling causes the next domino to fall so on and so forth. You can be the domino that helps another person change their mind and go from believing in free will to not believing in free will.

- Human beings are in and part of the cause and effect universe.
- Human beings cannot escape this simple concept of causality.
- Please help change one person's mind about this free will issue.

Very Truly Yours,
Nick Vale

Foreword - Part Two

In The Beginning . . .

Openly refuting "free will," will be the most important "taboo" subject matter ever discussed and debated in the history of time when it finally comes out of hiding. Enough with academia and philosophy class already. Let's bring this topic to the people (Main Street). The illusion of free will is so prevalent in our society that many people don't even know that they have been living all these years in a lie. Believing in free will is the mythical monster of the times we currently live in. This new kind of Bible (The Holy Bible: No Free Will) can prove and persuade you to the truth that free will doesn't exist. This book can also show you how a planet without free will is actually a better and more compassionate planet to live on.

Make this promise to yourself before you begin:

I am now going to look at the issue of "free will." Do we as human beings have the ability to make our own decisions in all matters of life? Is it left up to you and me to decide how our lives will be lived or it up to God (the entirety of the universe)?

We either have "free will" or we don't. Many people love to say they have "a little free will." A "little free will" means you do in fact believe in free will. This is a black or white issue. You either have free will or you don't.

We cannot have two truths fighting against each other; if two truths do fight against each other then what you have is not truth. There can only be one truth in this matter and it's about time to understand that free will doesn't exist and is categorically and axiomatically impossible.

Some people like to say that cause and effect doesn't apply to them because they are made of a non—material or non—physical spirit or soul.

There are two possibilities of a non-physical entity within you:

1) If there is a non-physical entity within you (soul or sprit), you are not in conscious control of it. Free Will is not saved.
2) Even if your non-physical entity is just an advisor of yours (trying to push you in one direction or another), free will is not saved. Your "advisor" just becomes part of your causal chain (chain of causality in one moment in time) just like any other person would be.

Either way:

- Non Physical causation (if you believe in such a thing) still must happen in a moment in time. Moments in time are linear as one moment in time is the cause of the next moment in time. So on and so forth.
- Conclusion: Free Will is not saved.

The Holy Bible: No Free Will. Amen.

Book One by The Steward

The Book of
Definition

Chapter One

BEFORE we begin, let me introduce you to what the term "free will" means.

"Free Will" Defined

The American Heritage College Dictionary:

"**free will** *n.* **1.** The ability or discretion to choose; free choice. **2.** The power of making free choices that are unconstrained by external circumstances or by an agency such as fate or divine will."

*Meriam-Webster Collegiate Dictionary/*Eleventh Edition:

"**free will** *n.* freedom of humans to make choices that are not determined by prior causes or by divine intervention."

2   It is useless to have a refutation of this term "free will" unless we define it first. As can be seen from our dictionaries, the term "free will" means the ability to make "free choices." Not just choices, but "free" choices.

3   Notice that our dictionaries are specific in stating that it is "free choice" that is the definition of "free will," rather than just "choice" alone. To be an expression of "free will," choices must also be free. Free from what? We just read it:

- Free from "prior causes."
- Free from "constraint."
- Free from "external circumstances."
- Free from "fate."
- Free from "divine will."
- Free from "divine intervention."

4   Those who would argue for free will, however, refuse being held to these precise and concise definitions. They want the mere ability to "make a choice" to be considered an act of "free will." Well it is nothing of the kind. Making a choice has absolutely nothing to do with the doctrine of "free will." This is easily demonstrated. Computers make "choices." They can make millions of "choices" per second. It would take a million people to make that many choices in a second. All that these marvelous machines do is make choices.

5   Now then, will anyone maintain that computers have unprogrammed and uncaused free wills? So now we have proof that making choices is not the same as "free will."

6   Computers do not have "free wills," yet they can make choices, but those choices are anything but free. Their choices are all a matter of pre-programming. They cannot think and act independently of their "causes" otherwise known as their programming or inputs. Neither can man think or do anything outside of the realm of his or her "causes," "programming," or "inputs." In order for an effect to be present, there must first be a cause, and once something is caused, the effect must follow, and neither could have been prevented.

7   There has not been one example ever created in the entire history of the entire universe that can be presented by any scientific method known to man (including Heisenberg's Uncertainty Principle) that can demonstrate that man's will is free from causality. Neither is there an example in all Scripture that can be shown to be the exercise of a will that is free from causality.
8   What is the difference between a partial preference and a full preference?

All preferences start with no preferences as we have no idea what we like and don't like. Take for example a baby boy who has never had a scoop of ice cream and is only presented with two choices -- a scoop of vanilla ice cream or a scoop of chocolate ice cream. He will most likely choose vanilla one time and chocolate one time (out of curiosity).

9   Preferences then go from a "no preference" state to a "partial preference" state. Back and forth we go until (as we get older) start picking vanilla slightly more often than chocolate.
10 Then eventually we go from a "partial preference" to a "full preference" (always picking vanilla) because we simply now know we enjoy that flavor much more than the other.
11 Preferences are built up over time as likes and dislikes become more apparent to oneself (but this also does not prove free will). In this example—we obviously did not choose our taste buds. Another example would be whether or not you prefer the window or aisle seat when you fly on an airplane.
12 Preferences do not prove free will. Preferences are built up over time and demonstrate/manifest genetic predispositions coming to fruition via actual life (interacting with one's environment). In the example above (as stated), we did not choose our taste buds.
13 Preferences simply highlight how cause and effect rule all of mankind and in fact prove that free will is just an illusion. When we choose something over something else, all we are doing is adhering to the "hedonic imperative" and move towards pleasure and away from pain (also known as pleasure principle).

14 Given the choice, why would you choose to sit in the aisle seat if you knew you much preferred the window seat? And while sitting in the window seat (your full preference), given the choice, why you would order chocolate ice cream if you knew you much preferred vanilla? The answer is you wouldn't (hedonic imperative).
15 Just because human beings most often do what they want to do does not give them free will. In other words, even though it's true you hardly ever do anything against your will (your wants/desires), you still do not have free will. This is because we most often can do what we want/desire to do, but we cannot choose what we want/desire to do.

- Human Beings are human computers that are programmed to always go toward pleasure and away from pain. There is no choice in the matter.

16 Another definition of Free Will: You/they could have done otherwise.

- Rest assured, if you/they could have done otherwise, you/they would have done otherwise.

The Holy Bible: No Free Will. Amen.

Book Two by The Introducer

The Book of

Introduction

Chapter One

WHAT are some of the benefits of understanding that free will is a myth? For starters excessive pride and arrogance will go away because you are not fundamentally praiseworthy since everything that you do or that was done to you was fated. This also eliminates excessive blame towards yourself and others as neither they nor you could have altered the course of whatever has happened to you in the past.

2   When you deeply blame and resent someone or something, what you are really saying is "they should have been able to rise above their circumstances and conditioning and done the 'right thing' by me. All they had to do was simply make use of their 'free will' and behave like a 'good' person. Since they didn't choose to act that way, they are a 'bad' person."

3   When a baby is born, we all know that the baby could not have a free will and needs to be taught everything about life.

4   So when exactly would free will start? At what age? 6? 12? 16? 19?

5. And if it did start suddenly out of nowhere -- how would you know? How could you tell? What would the signs be?
6. What would "free will" suddenly look like?
7. We humans are not acknowledging a fundamental truth about our existence when we believe in a free will.
8. As a species we owe it to ourselves to get this right once and for all.
9. This will create a planet of more compassion and understanding towards our fellow man as we all begin to evolve consciously to a place where we can all talk about what we are experiencing here more accurately.
10. In the future, the humans of a not too distant tomorrow, will consider us in the "dark ages" of consciousness and will find it almost comical that it took us this long to finally realize free will doesn't exist.
11. On the other hand, they won't be able to judge us for we had no choice in the matter as to how, why, or when the free will illusion bubble will finally burst.
12. Free will's illusory bubble will pop and burst when it's meant to be (just like everything else in life).
13. It's in the hands of fate as I write this.
14. As you go through life, you will constantly be conditioned by experiences and information.
15. You will make choices that are not free, but are based on prior information, conditioning, and determinants.
16. Free will implies that there are choices in life that are exactly 50/50. To be clear that means 50.000000 to infinity versus 50.000000 also to infinity. That's simply impossible.
17. Nothing is ever exactly 50/50. By this I mean two choices are never exactly equal. One choice will inevitably seem "better" to us after a good long while of thinking about it.
18. This is not because we have a free will. This is simply because we have a conditioned preference built up inside us over time.

"This Holy Bible of No Free Will is not about the illusion of making choices. We know we make choices. This is about the illusion of free will."

—The Introducer

19 Once we go through the process of living and thinking, we will always inevitably find one choice is better for us than the others.
20 A 50/50 choice would make us in essence a "first causer" which would make us a little God.
21 In other words, all decisions were and are inevitable once we go through the process of actually living.
22 Just because we do not possess a free will does not mean we cannot enjoy the already made movie that is our life.
23 This is because there are so many twists and turns and so many unexpected things that happen to us, that we soon realize the joy of living is how the story unfolds (how the story is told is why we go to the movies).
24 The best story tellers are the best movies and vice versa.

"There are only two types of people in the world. Those who believe in free will and those who do not. There is no grey area or wiggle room. I had no choice but to state that."

—The Introducer

25 Attraction isn't a choice. As humans, we don't "consciously choose" who we feel attracted to. It just "happens" to us . . . Bang! And you can't "convince" someone to feel this powerful emotion.
26 Attraction doesn't make logical sense (so much of our conditioning is stored in our unconscious/subconscious).
27 When you think about the concept of being attracted to another person (physically or emotionally), it only "makes sense" that you should feel attracted to good qualities like "kindness," "honesty," and "loyalty," right?
28 Then why do we fall for people who lack everything we say we are looking for?
29 A human's lack of free will is most apparent in the dating world. Nobody would choose to suddenly fall out of love with someone.
30 Nobody would choose to get a divorce if it were up to them.

31 Attraction clearly isn't freely willed. There is no logical sense to who we are attracted to and who we are not attracted to. Call it timing. Call it chemical. Call it biological. Call it fate.
32 Whatever you call it, it certainly cannot be called "free" will.

"We are on the verge of a huge breakthrough. The widespread knowledge that man does not possess a free will tipping point is coming very soon."

—The Introducer

The Holy Bible: No Free Will. Amen.

Book Three by Nick Vale

The Book of

Understanding

Chapter One

SUCH things as increasing rates of depression, violence, suicide, wars, revolutions, self-hatred, other hatred, self-blame, other blame, political turmoil, and natural disasters are all symptoms of a planet in a downward spiral.

2. The total cumulative sum effort of all previous generations to build, create, and invest in making our individual journeys through life an overall more peaceful and pleasant experience (while well intended) seem to have failed us miserably.
3. This is because in spite of all the so-called advances and progressions we have made in such things as technology (thereby increasing the overall material standard of living), it seems we have made very little to no progress at all in the most important aspect of being a human being -- the evolution of human consciousness.
4. The so-called progress we have made in the material world has not been progress at all.

5   It seems that under the "free will" model after every progression (cell phones, email, internet etc.), we have had to go back to try and try again to fulfill ourselves with newer and faster models of everything often resulting in less and less life satisfaction.
6   We find ourselves reverting back to the old habits of feeling empty and lost as crucial life lessons remain elusive and unlearned time and time again.
7   In other words, overall life satisfaction is not increasing even though all these technological advances would suggest otherwise.
8   Why is this?

It is the basic belief of The Holy Bible: No Free Will that upon proper reflection of life, the future of the planet, and each individual's contribution (however small it may be), that the basic foundation of society's collective consciousness is incorrect.

9   This basic foundational consciousness error on the smallest of levels (butterfly effect) creates a massive outward ripple effect causing more and more untold human misery.
10 It will only continue to get worse and worse unless something new and different comes along and changes the underlying way we collectively perceive and understand the world in which we live in.
11 In short, our collective consciousness or the way we view things simply needs to change because it is currently incorrect (the belief in free will).
12 While it may be difficult to believe at first, it is quite possible that the force of energy emanating from the cataclysmic "big bang," or from any other story of creation may have in fact created a cause and effect chain that predestined the very moment of our birth, every move that we make, every pattern of our existence, every thought that we have, and even the exact moment of our death.
13 This is of course hypothetical speculation just as much as "free will" is hypothetical speculation.

14 Neither is provable, but it is indeed time to understand that one version of this story is much more likely than the other -- that so-called "free will" is an illusion, and just a myth.
15 The "free will" model of reality has had enough time to be tried and tested, and it simply no longer makes any logical sense to believe in such a thing.
16 The results of new neuroscience data are now in, and the belief in "free will" simply no longer makes any logical sense.
17 The "unfree will" model is actually much more logical and easier to prove.
18 This new kind of Holy Bible: No Free Will believes that humans now possess the intellectual capacity to understand how and why it is much more likely and logical that a human's will is completely and utterly one hundred percent causal (meaning "unfree"), and that all of life is therefore predetermined.
19 The Holy Bible: No Free Will explains the basic premise that man does not possess a "free will," and why this is very good news for society's future.
20 A better world is envisioned as the basic premise that everything has a cause will begin to be implemented into daily life.
21 Quite frankly, it is time to try something different. The free will model is simply not working. Look at how much hatred and despair our planet currently has.
22 Let's create a society based on the correct foundation of reality --that man's will simply is not free.
23 We believe the results of a one hundred percent causal will society cannot be any worse than the world we currently live in (so we have nothing to lose).
24 We believe the results of an unfree will society will be far better.
25 We envision a much more understanding and compassionate world.
26 All we are asking from you, the reader, is to keep an open mind and give a whole new way of life a chance.
27 This book challenges traditional thinking and forces people to reconsider their notion of "free" will and see their entire self-image in a whole new context.

28 The Holy Bible: No Free Will consists of an evolving theory hoping to explain how lives are lead in reality. The reality is this -- Man's Will Is Not Free. Amen.

29 Everything that is or is not must be as it is or is not and everything must be as it is, or it would be otherwise. That includes your current belief or disbelief in free will.

30 Everything is happening exactly as it was meant to be throughout the entire universe, from the smallest subatomic particle to the largest and most remote galaxy. Each human life is a small but necessary element of the entire universe. Individual choices are always caused and it doesn't matter how they are caused. The "I Am" that we are is just a witness to the mind/body as it manifests the will of God (aka the entire universe).

The Holy Bible: No Free Will. Amen.

Chapter Two

ON an entirely separate issue, this new kind of Bible of No Free Will feels that most if not all other "self-help" books or recovery programs make one very faulty assumption -- that human beings have a free will.

2. These books or recovery programs are conveniently easy to read, have simple titles, have simple rules or skills to learn and usually have a few simple steps or a certain amount of days to follow the author's instructions before the desired goal is achieved.
3. These books or recovery programs have simplistic titles like "The Seven Spiritual Laws of Success, Secrets of The Millionaire Mind, The Twelve Steps to Sobriety, The A, B, C method of Cognitive Behavior Therapy (rebt), The Thirty Day Money Workbook, or The DBT (dialectical behavior therapy) skills workbook."
4. As stated above, all these recovery programs seem to make the same very faulty assumption -- that human beings have something called "free will" and can just conveniently learn or not learn whatever they want or don't want whenever they want.
5. The authors of these books or recovery programs seem to believe that if we just tried hard enough and followed their twelve steps, went to their seminars or forums (the landmark forum comes to mind), mastered their DBT skills manual, or properly learned their A, B, Cs of cognitive behavior therapy *(REBT), we are all practically guaranteed a happy and healthy life.

*rational emotive behavior therapy (REBT) and all cognitive behavior therapy is based on being "rational"

*"There is nothing more irrational than believing in free will."

—Nick Vale

6. The main DBT (dialectical behavior therapy) goal or concept is to "build a life worth living."

"If everyone could freely will a life worth living, they would. With free will, nobody would ever fail at DBT, yet so many people do."

—Nick Vale

7. If we all had this magical thing called "free will" then why do some of us fail time and time again to attain such things as mental, physical, material, emotional and spiritual health?
8. Nobody would ever fail at The Twelve Steps, Cognitive Behavior Therapy (CBT), REBT, or DBT (dialectical behavior therapy) if we had a free will.
9. Everyone who has taken such things as a DBT course would simply learn the skills supposedly needed to feel better.
10. The success rate would be 100%.
11. But not everyone "gets it" no matter how hard they try.
12. Who would ever choose to be depressed? How come some people in dialectical behavior therapy (for borderline personality disorder) get well, while others do not?
13. Most, if not all, recovery programs are condensed, written for, and marketed to the "mass market" consumer who just wants some easy steps or skills to follow to attain a certain goal (make more money, lose weight, become less depressed for example).
14. If we all had free wills then these "easy steps" or skills we needed to learn, or simplistic A, B, C paradigms to health (REBT) would all be easily attainable as we could all just freely will ourselves to learn them all.
15. The intellectual or super-intellectual (who is aware that free will is impossible) is always left out of the equation for some reason -- until now.
16. We feel this book, this new kind of Bible, includes all of mankind.
17. The Holy Bible: No Free Will has been written for the regular and average person as well as the intellectual or super intellectual.
18. The Holy Bible: No Free Will has teachings which are very complex and also tries to simplify things wherever and whenever possible.

"If humans had a free will they would be able to side step their brain's programming. People's desires, thoughts, actions, and beliefs would be completely independent of one's genes, memories, environment, and conditioning. All humans would be then left to flounder in a chaotic sea of total and complete indecision. 'What shall I do next? I can't make up my mind' would rule each of our moment to moment lives. We would all be little Gods and be first causers. As a powerful first causer we would all become paralyzed with indecision, confusion, emptiness, meaninglessness, and purposelessness. With 'free will' our super intelligent genetic code and personal experiences would now be completely erased, and we wouldn't have a clue of what to do next because we would no longer know what we'd prefer doing in any given situation or circumstance."

—Nick Vale

"Openly refuting the existence of free will has been a taboo subject for many years now. In fact, I don't think I've ever seen a talk show debating this issue on television or heard one on the radio. Buckle your seat belts people because this is all about to change in a huge way. The free will is an illusion tipping point is coming to a town or city near you real soon. The truth is on the way and will sell like hotcakes. Salesmen/women will not be needed because the truth easily sells itself."

—Nick Vale

The Holy Bible: No Free Will. Amen.

Book Four by Nick Vale

The Book of

The Word "Free" Confuses

Chapter One

An example of how we know free will doesn't exist:

People in different countries speak different languages and people in different regions of different countries speak with different dialects.

This is one of many reasons why the belief in free will is total, complete, utter insanity and nonsense.

The problem is the word "free"
What does the word "free" mean?
Let's look at some common ways the word free is used in the world today. It's very confusing to say the least.

- The word free is confusing

Free riding
Free loading
Buy one get one Free

There is no Free lunch
It's a Free country
I have Freedom of speech
Land of the Free
Freeway
I'm a Free man
I'm Free to do whatever I want
Chlorine Free
Sugar Free
Germ Free
Get out of jail Free card
Free as a bird
Free falling
Free Range
Free Throw (Basketball term)
Live Free or die (State of New Hampshire License Plate)
I feel so wild and Free
I'm Free Saturday night for dinner
I own that Free and clear
The quarterback somehow avoided the sack and got Free
Free at last, Free at last, thank God Almighty, I'm Free at last
I choose, therefore I have Free will
I'm pain Free
I'm home Free
Free parking

There's no charge. It's Free.
If you love someone, set them Free
Political Freedom
Freedom Tower
I'm independently wealthy and Free to do whatever I so desire
With Liberty and justice for all
Life, Liberty and the pursuit of happiness
Let Freedom Ring
The Statue of Liberty
The Liberty Bell

2   The many ways in which we use the word free in the English language is partly the reason why so many people incorrectly believe they have a free will.
3   Let's make this very clear:

Human beings are not "free" to do whatever they want, whenever they want because our actions are causally bound (chain of events).

4   If a dear and respected friend or family member recommended something to you (say a movie), you will most likely go see it.
5   This is called "word of mouth" advertising and is the most effective type of advertising out there. The suggestion or recommendation caused you to do a certain action.
6   This is not "free" will. This is simply a cause creating an action.
7   Now that you've begun to read The Holy Bible: No Free Will think about what the cause or causes were for you to pick up this book in the first place.
8   Now think about what the word "free" means to you.

What are you seeking by reading this book? You are probably seeking self-realization, truth, and enlightenment. But you are actually not doing anything at all.

9   You may be the thinker of your thoughts, and the experiencer of your experiences, but you are not self—creating them to occur.
10 They just happen as the cause and effect chain (think of a train) keeps deterministically barreling through space and time. "The Choo! Choo! Train of the Causal Chain."
11 You see every moment of the train's movement is directly dependent on the moment of the train's movement the moment before.
12 This is just like your life. Every moment of your life is dependent on the moment before, no exceptions.
13 This is quite easy to understand as every moment of the universe is dependent on the moment before and human beings are part of the universe.
14 "All aboard the Truth Express. Choo! Choo!"

15   There is no credible evidence to support the notion of a "free" will. What would a "free" will decision even look like?
16   It would have to be totally independent of anything that has ever influenced, been taught, or suggested to you. Independent of your biology (genetics) and environment. Independent of your nature and nurture.
17   Yes you can live quite well knowing that free will is a myth, an illusion. You won't blame people as much nor will you blame yourself as much.
18   You will see reality as it really is -- just a bunch of conditioned people walking around making decisions and manifesting their past experiences (past conditioning, and genetics).
19   No free will should equal less animosity and acrimony towards ourselves and others as we learn to accept that everything was, is, and will be fated and predetermined.
20   A planet without free will should be a much better planet to live on.
21   The Holy Bible: No Free Will aims to bring goodness and light to this previously taboo subject.
22   Human beings simply do and say what they have been taught to do and say in any given situation or do and say what they feel will give them the most pleasure or least pain in any given situation.
23   People get trained ("Choo! Choo!) just like animals do except we are a million times more complicated and have a sub/unconscious.
24   Many people make decisions which appear to be uncaused because the cause is unknown to them. This is because the cause is in the sub/unconscious.
25   The Brain is the actual chooser.

"My quarks made me do it." Your brain allows you to choose a Volkswagen or a BMW for example.

26   Is that free will? You choose one thing over another due to preferences not because you have a free will.
27   Preferences develop over time as a pattern in brain neuro chemistry which is completely dependent on past experiences.

28 Eventually, one pattern passes a certain criteria test for the brain which allows you to choose something over another.
29 It allows you to pick a pizza over a hot dog for example and a trip to Spain over a trip to France. Choosing is an extremely complex, cerebral event.
30 Our brains can store millions of emotional memories, past decisions, and ultimately gives us a "feeling" or an intuition or a "hunch" to do or purchase one item or brand over another.
31 People say "it just felt or feels right" or "it just felt like the right thing to do at the time."
32 Contrary to public belief -- you can't think whatever you want to think about anything.
33 In fact your entire life is predetermined and everything was meant to be exactly the way it is now and will be in the future.
34 The experience of choosing is a neural process, with the obvious function of selecting a behavior with its reasonable and foreseeable consequences. It responds to information from the senses, including the recommendations, suggestions, advice, and warnings from other people.
35 You cannot step outside your conditioning no matter how hard you may try.
36 From the moment of your conception, your neural grooves began to be honed like an old vinyl record album. Neuro synapses in your brain and throughout your entire body began to form and strengthen. The more you repeated an action, thought or motion, the stronger they became.
37 Some you were born with, some you have acquired throughout your lifetime and some you will continue to acquire as you go through life on the "Truth Express."
38 The causal chain is the mightiest train of all. "Choo! Choo!"
39 You cannot escape outside the realm of your genetic automatic responses (reflexes) or learned responses by simply "letting them go" or "willing them away." However, one day you may wake up and say, "I need to change my conditioning." How did that happen?

"What a train of thought that last verse was."

—Nick Vale

40   Well since every moment of the universe is dependent on the moment before and humans are no exception, then clearly what has happened to your brain state is that "the moment before" was a "moment" in which you realized that you were ready to become aware that your conditioning processes needed to be changed.
41   You had conditioned yourself to believe that you were in need of re-conditioning. It's still all part of the same causal chain because causal chains can never be broken even if you "choose" to change you conditioning patterns.
42   You might decide for example to only reward yourself if you "do well" at something. You might also decide to punish yourself if you "screw something up."
43   Either way -- the time had come for these thoughts and this has nothing to do with man having a "free will."

"Deciding to change one's conditioning is just a moment in time (new thought) dependent on the moment in time before that moment in time (thought before new thought). It has nothing to do with having a free will. Choo! Choo!"

—Nick Vale

"Making a decision does not mean we have a free will even if that decision is to change one's conditioning. All decisions are dependent on the moment before just like how every moment of the universe is dependent on the moment before."

—Nick Vale

"Human decision making is never uncaused and we are not first or self-causers."

—Nick Vale

- We do not have Free Wills. We have internally caused (how all stimuli makes us feel on the inside) personal history wills. In other words and to be crystal clear—how all internal and/or external, physical and/or non-physical, material and/or nonmaterial causes/stimuli makes us feel _on the inside_. Amen.
- **It does not matter how things are caused** (physical or non-physical causation). **The point is everything has to have a cause**. Everything we do has a history of reasons (psychological/emotional causes). Amen.

The Holy Bible: No Free Will. Amen.

Book Five by Nick Vale

The Book of

The Illusion of Free Will

Chapter One

THE illusion of free will surrounds us like the air we breathe or the water that the fish live in. The fish have no idea that they even live in water. They just do. It's just all around them all the time and it's all they know. People often say such things as "I did this and that." "He did this or that. "He went to the store." "He sold his business." "He built his business from scratch." "He scored a touchdown." "She ran for her life." "She made all the right moves." For practical, pragmatic, and useful reasons this is all fine and dandy, but at some point the fundamental truth about human reality needs to be addressed.

2. Our language is so embedded with the free will assumption, it is a miracle anyone doesn't believe in a free will.
3. To my utter amazement, I am finding more and more people each day understanding and realizing that free will is just a myth, an illusion.
4. The bubble will burst on this free will thing, it's just a matter of time. Life can be just as amazing and wonderful once you realize you don't have a free will.

"Cause and Effect is the most beautiful two step dance ever invented in the history of the world. If you cannot figure out why free will is impossible, you haven't correctly analyzed what is actually being done during this two- step dance. This dance was invented at the beginning of time and will keep dancing into infinity."

—Nick Vale

"I've yet to discover how anyone with any real and meaningful intelligence could actually believe that human beings have free will. In my opinion its super obvious that we don't."

—Nick Vale

5   The Heisenberg Principle, Uncertainty Principle, Copenhagen Interpretation, (whatever you want to call it), proved that everything is random, probabilistic, or that there are still hidden variables not yet discovered.
6   The one thing it didn't prove is that man has a "free will."

"All human choices are constrained by many causes. The vast majority of people believe they have a free will because they experience **the feeling of** *making a choice. If I have* **the feeling** *that I am a rock star, does that make me a rock star?"*

—Nick Vale

- Not only is Free Will just an illusory feeling. It's also a faulty conclusion.
- Your actions are strict causal outcomes of your nature and nurture. Free Will is nowhere to be found.

7   The debate as to the ultimate causes of human action has been at the core of Western philosophy for centuries.
8   Most of this debate centers upon what constitutes freedom of action, and whether an individual has the capacity to choose between alternatives.

9 Although there are numerous derivatives of these approaches, they can generally be divided into two overarching theories of human behavior: free will and determinism.

10 Free will theory contends that human behavior, when faced with a given situation, is the result of individual choices made by autonomous actors.

11 The theory assumes that individuals are unique actors -- they have an inherent ability to choose or "choose not" when confronted with specific environmental stimuli.

12 It thus follows that, with this choice, individuals can be held personally responsible for their choices, and thus should face the consequences for their decisions.

13 In contrast, determinist theory sees human behavior quite differently. Determinists contend that individual action is "caused" by factors outside of an individual's control. Determinists believe all of life is causal (meaning ruled by cause and effect) and that all of life is a conditioned response.

14 These causal forces might range from divine intervention to interactions between social and biological factors. But, whatever they are, they compel human behavior. All determinists share the common belief that individual behavior cannot be separated from causal forces.

15 All the authors of this new kind of Holy Bible, The Holy Bible: No Free Will are strict determinists and quality of life researchers. We are also known as incompatibilists (in philosophy) because we believe free will and determinism are not compatible. We believe people who do not believe in the nonsense of free will, can have much better lives. People can still be depressed, but they will no longer be depressed that they are depressed. People can still be angry, but they will no longer be angry that they are angry. People will of course still feel upset and/or sad, but they will no longer be upset and/or sad that they are upset and/ or sad. People will still be fallible and fail at things, but will no longer feel the secondary emotion of being upset and/or sad with themselves that they are fallible and fail at things.

- Choices are never exactly 50/50.
- You are not in control of your feelings.
- Even if there were a choice that was exactly 50/50, you did not choose how intelligent you are.
- The mental health profession is all about sanity. The mental health profession is in need of an entire overhaul. There is nothing more insane than believing man has free will.
- Free Will is a very harmful and toxic belief. It makes people feel like failures when they fail at something.

The Holy Bible: No Free Will. Amen.

Book Six by The Absorber

The Book of

How It All Works

Chapter One

VANILLA or chocolate?

We go into an ice cream store and choose Vanilla over Chocolate. It is a seemingly simple choice, and we claim that our taste preference is the cause of this choice. Yet choices are never that simple.

"We can choose our preferences, but we cannot choose what we prefer."

—The Absorber

2   The choice of Vanilla is influenced not only by taste, but also by color, texture, smell, presentation, and more than likely by earlier pleasant memories of the flavor Vanilla.

3   Compared to other decisions we make in life, deciding which flavor of ice cream to order is a relatively simple one.

4   Other decisions or undertakings such as strategies in war, whether to marry or not, to leave one's job or not, to learn how to play a very complex computer game (or the guitar), take

complexity that will involve a multitude of multifaceted mental/brain activity, and often interrelated calculations of muscle brain memory, degree of strength, distances, time, ratios, speed of movement and towards what direction, and which fingers/toes to use.

5   Hand eye coordination synapses have to be fired off, and neurotransmitters are set off in every conceivable way. All in a micro-second.
6   Neuroscience is forcing us to reconsider all this complexity in a more simplified way. It is simple actually.
7   Every moment of every action is dependent on the moment before no matter how complex.
8   One moment in time causes the next moment in time. So on and so forth.
9   Pleasure brings about a certain response in the future (more likely to do again) and pain does the same exact thing (more likely to avoid the next time).
10 Once again "act as if" you have a free will on a practical and pragmatic human level.
11 On the fundamental God Level of Ultimate Truth -- we cannot be ultimately responsible for our behavior.
12 According to the books of this newer testament known as The Holy Bible: No Free Will -- while it may be of great pragmatic value to hold people responsible for their actions, and to employ systems of reward and punishment, no one fundamentally is really deserving of blame or praise for anything. Welcome to the age of "blameless responsibility."

The Holy Bible: No Free Will. Amen.

Chapter Two

CAUSAL chains

A causal chain is a series of causes leading to an effect. We cannot know all of the causes of our choices in any one chain (thanks to the sub/unconscious), but we can know the cause and effect of a few obvious leading causes.

2   For example:

I got drunk and that's why I got into a car accident

But why did you have the need/desire to drink and drive in the first place?

3. Obvious Causes: Causes we can know. We can readily spot one or a few causes for an event. I parked at a fire hydrant. I got a parking ticket.
4. Hidden Causes: Causes we can't know. Most of them happened before we were even born, like the impact on your life by the Ottoman Empire, Marco Polo, or Alexander the Great. As stated before, most of the reasons and causes behind our choices are hiding in our sub/unconscious. This is a concept that was popularized by Sigmund Freud.
5. False Causes: Unrelated and improvable causes. This is when we rationalize what we have done in retrospect and just start making stuff up so that it fits neatly into our life paradigm. But we have no proof of it causing anything and invent it after the fact (to make some sense of it all).
6. Most people believe they have free will because they choose things. As we have stated choosing does not equal free will. Choosing nonetheless, is a very real human experience, and we do it a hundred times a day (at least) consciously and mostly unconsciously.
7. Our choices propel us from one place to another, enable us to get our needs met, and give us the feeling that we are creating our lives.

8   The choosing process usually goes something like this:

Step 1

Options arise. We consider the costs and consequences, pros and cons etc. We always want to pick the option and/or options that will bring us the most pleasure and least pain.

Step 2

We select one or more option(s)

As the option(s) becomes stronger and more desirable than the others, we make a choice. Our intuition often guides us.

Step 3

We act on our choice

Step 4

We judge the results of our choice. This is how and why we will decide in the future to make the same choice or not if the same situation or set of circumstances were to occur. We live and learn by reflecting on our choices and if we experienced a painful outcome we now know for the next time to choose differently.

9   What if we don't make a decision?

Then we have simply made a choice to not make a choice (so it is therefore still a choice).

10 Some people say that their soul or spirit made the choice for them.

"How does having a soul or spirit choosing on my behalf give me a free will? That doesn't sound like I'm in control of anything. In fact, a non-physical mysterious entity choosing on my behalf would make me feel more out of control than ever."

—The Absorber

11 My Spirit or Soul makes my decisions for me:

A non-physical entity coming completely out of left field without any reasoning behind it? On top of that, why doesn't the spirit/soul get conditioned and learn from its mistakes just like every other organ/system we have?

12 Now, let's say your decision making has led you to experience incredible amounts of pain in your lifetime. Rest assured, if you could have done it differently -- you would have. You made the best decision you could with the knowledge you had at that particular moment in time. If you knew a building was going to collapse onto you and kill you before you ran into it to save people would you still have run in there and sacrificed your life?

If yes, why? If no, why not?

13 While it's true that you can improve upon your performance the next time, you're in a similar situation, you can never repeat the past. You can't put your toe in the water the exact same way twice. This is because there are so many moving parts and variables that occur during the passage of time.
14 What you will do the next time is make the best decision you can with the new knowledge you have at that new particular moment in time (acquired from reflecting on the results of how well you did or didn't do the last time). This is the karmic stream of life.
15 In closing everything that happens has a cause. Everything you think, say, and do happen because something preceded it. Nothing can appear without being brought about, created, or formed by antecedents or precursors.

16 Furthermore, every effect becomes a cause. Effects don't just lounge around all day without a purpose, cut class, smoke pot, play video games and go into hiding. They do just the opposite.
17 Effects are straight A students with 4.0 GPA's. They very skillfully hover around you like an invisible armada of protective helicopters or hummingbirds making sure your prior mistakes are not repeated. They protect you from making the same exact mistake twice (if they can help it). They provoke other new decisions into action so that history won't repeat itself.
18 Mistakes want you to have learned your lesson(s). The effects of prior causes (your feelings after the past decisions you have made) are extremely powerful creators of new decisions to be made at a time in the future when their relevance is most relied upon.
19 Cause and effect are two sides of the same decision coin that are stored up in our memory banks (consciously and/or sub/unconsciously) that keep influencing our decision making so on and so forth until the day we die.

The Holy Bible: No Free Will. Amen.

Book Seven by The Causer

The Book of

Law Of Causation

Chapter One

IT is generally believed that our sense of free will presents an interesting dilemma: on the one hand, it is difficult to make sense of it in purely causal terms; on the other hand, we *feel as if we are the* creators of our own actions.

2   It's like asking what came first the chicken or the egg? I think that this confusion is in itself a symptom of our dilemma. We are going about this all wrong. If free will is in fact a grand illusion then our entire investigative process into this matter is distorted to begin with. It's like trying to figure out a magic trick in a hallway full of smoke and mirrors.

3   Our experience is not merely delivering a distorted view of reality, but it is also creating the faulty way in which we go about in trying to discover the truth. This is why for many years I have read many authors and philosophers debate the issue.

4   I have found time and time again, they all practice the art of "confusionism" (as in a total state of confusion) or circular reasoning. This means all they do is confuse people when the

answer is actually so very simple. They love to tell people "you have free will" yet "God is in control of everything." Well, which is it? Pick a side for once. Stop the free will flip flopping and double talk insanity. Let's be crystal clear. You do not have a free will. Period. Clear enough?

5 All we have to do in order to unravel this do I or don't I have a free will question is simply pay very close attention to what it is like to be ourselves in the world. For example, look at the manifesto written by *Elliot Rodger. It's all cause and effect and shows how he had neither control over his causes (how hurt and alone he felt) nor his effects (his subsequent anger and rage). What came first? the chicken or the egg type of debating gets everybody confused and all of us back to square one with nothing accomplished. Did I cause that or did that cause me will now mercifully end.

- *"All I ever wanted was to fit in and live a happy life amongst humanity, but I was cast out and rejected, forced to endure an existence of loneliness and insignificance all be**cause** . . . I didn't want things to turn out this way, but humanity **forced my hand**, and this story will explain why . . . I didn't ask for this. I didn't want this."
- Since Elliot Rodger knew he was "twisted" and even titled his manifesto "My Twisted World" why didn't he stop himself? Answer: No Free Will
- Also on page 109 Elliot says "I couldn't believe my life was actually turning out this way." He expresses surprise to find himself at a gun shooting range planning a massacre. He couldn't believe that he was actually beginning to plan for his "day of retribution." Why was he surprised to be there you ask if he was the one wanting to be there? How could he be surprising himself you ask? After all nobody was forcing him to be there right? Right and wrong. No one person was forcing him to be there **but he was compelled by the entirety of the universe to be there**. He was just a witness to his own life and he knew it (hence his surprise that things were "actually turning out this way").

- Being just a witness to our own life is true for all of us. We are all compelled by the big bang (or any other story of creation) to do what we have to do. We are all just along for the ride playing out our assigned roles. Conclusion: No Free Will.

6. The moment we do pay attention, very close attention, we begin to see that free will is **just a feeling**. No more, no less. The illusion of free will is just that, an illusion. All one needs to do to get to the bottom of this seemingly complex issue is to understand the very simple law of causation. The "causal chain" rules all of mankind. Everything has a cause. Whether or not you are conscious of the cause or causes is an entirely separate issue (see the book by The Unconscious).

7. People who believe in free will, incorrectly believe that voluntary behavior (as opposed to mandated behavior) can actually occur...but how? They insist that free will means that man must be the "ultimate" or "originating" cause of his actions. He must be a **causa sui,** in the traditional phrase. To be responsible for one's choices is to be the first cause of those choices, where first cause means that there is no antecedent cause of that cause. The argument, then, is that if man has free will, then man is the ultimate cause of his actions. So are we back to what came first the chicken or the egg? No.

8. No we are not. Once again and in simple terms -- the law of causation reigns supreme. There is no need to argue with philosophy professors or academic types any longer. All they will do is confuse you and practice the art of "confusionism" on you. Circular reasoning, not philosophy, appears to be their real specialty. Philosophy professors invariably begin to wonder: did I cause that or did that cause me? What came first? Who's on first?

9. If predeterminism or simply put determinism is true, then all of man's choices are caused by events and feelings that were there before he made his choice not after.

10. The law of causation is that simple. The only question is what was the first cause? That nobody will ever know. What we do know however is that man was not the first cause because

humans were not part of the universe before it was created (or if it's been here forever and ever). The universe is way older than mankind.

11 We were either created through such things as the story of creation or evolution. We simply weren't here first to cause anything in any scenario. So, if everything man does is caused by events, facts, and feelings outside his control, then he cannot by definition be the ultimate self - causer of his thoughts, feelings, beliefs, and actions.

12 All the relevant features of a person's inner life such as emotions cause behaviors. Again it's quite a simple equation. Beliefs = thoughts = emotions = behaviors. So where do the beliefs come from? Once again -- the law of causation is the answer.

13 Causality is the relationship between an event (the *cause*) and a second event (the *effect*), where the second event is understood as a consequence of the first. We are not born with beliefs or a belief system. Beliefs are taught to us once we are born by such methods as modeling others (for example our parents), verbally taught to us, or a myriad of other ways we form our "paradigm" or belief system about the world.

14 So even though I may not be able to know exactly where or why my beliefs or thoughts come to me as they do (don't forget about the sub/unconscious), I can rest in the peace and knowledge that something has caused them to be the way they are due to the law of causation.

15 The sub/unconscious is also always at play here, so that is yet another reason why we cannot pinpoint with accuracy where or why our thoughts are the way they are. Just because you don't know exactly what the cause or causes are for your behavior(s), doesn't mean they don't exist. They do. It's just that you don't know what they are, that's all.

16 Many people seem to feel that quantum mechanics has liberated the human mind from the prison of determinism. They say there is proof that in quantum mechanics of uncaused effects.

17 I say that is impossible. There are only two answers to this quantum mechanics/physics argument. One -- there are hidden variables not yet discovered causing the outcomes to be what

they are (remember the last quark was only discovered around 27 years ago and the Higgs Boson was also recently discovered).

Isn't it extremely arrogant to think that we've discovered all the subatomic particles that could ever be and that there will be no new discoveries forthcoming? For example in 2022: google new discovery of exotic particles include the pentaquark and tetraquark. Or Two -- everything is random. If everything is random that still doesn't mean we have free will.

So as far as the Quantum Mechanics argument goes The Holy Bible: No Free Will has two answers and here they are:

#1 *hidden variables not yet discovered proving determinism true
or
#2 everything is random

Either way. No Free Will. Amen

*Gerard't Hooft (Nobel Prize in Physics 1999) also firmly believes that there should be a deterministic theory underlying quantum mechanics.

Now back to causality.

18. Let's look at a real world example: You go over to your friend's house and he accidently falls down a flight of stairs and loses consciousness. He's barely breathing. You then begin to frantically call 911 for help. You rush to his side feeling an intense desire to help.
19. Your "self" now seems to stand at the intersection of what to do and what not to do. Should you try CPR? Do you take his pulse to see if it's normal? Should you put him in your car and rush him to the hospital or wait for the ambulance? Should you call your next door neighbor who you know is a doctor?
20. From this point of view, one can easily see how **one can feel as if** he is the lone source of his own thoughts and actions. You need to quickly decide on what to do and what not to do.
21. You **seem to be an agent acting** of your own free will. The problem is that this point of view cannot be reconciled with what we know about the human brain.

22 We now know that every moment your brain is dependent on the moment before. This basically means you are trained in certain things and not trained in others. Do you even know how to do CPR? Do you even know how to take someone's pulse? Do you even know what a normal pulse rate would feel and sound like?

23 You see, what are your causes? What have you been taught in the past? What have you been told? Practiced? Trained in? What or which neuro-pathway grooves in your brain have been created? All these prior causes will determine what you do in such a crisis as stated above.

24 This is your skill set under pressure basically. You have skill sets that you have learned and built up over time. Some skill sets you can access under pressure and others you cannot. Some skill sets help people survive under the harshest of circumstances while others perish.

25 The ones who perish simply didn't have the skill set to survive that particular circumstance. To be clear and to simplify, our behavior can be traced to biological events happening in the synapses of our brains. The law of causation is the first and only law needed to understand why free will is an illusion.

26 Randomness: If I were to learn that my decision to take the bus this morning was due to a random release of neurotransmitters in my brain (as opposed to walking which I do 99.9% of the time), how could the indeterminacy of the initiating event count as me exercising my free will?

27 Such indeterminacy, if it were generally effective throughout my brain, would completely destroy any semblance of human responsibility. Say while on that bus, another random release of neurotransmitters in my brain were set off and I attacked the bus driver while we were in motion.

28 This indeterminacy of totally random behavior of me now attacking the bus driver will most likely cause a terrible accident. Say this terrible accident killed twenty-five people (but not myself). Obviously, the loved ones of the deceased would "blame" me because I'm the one who attacked the bus driver and caused the accident in the first place.

29 It is safe to say I will be going to jail for a very long time or might even face the death penalty for such a heinous crime. But if I could prove that my behavior was due to a random release of neurotransmitters in my brain -- how could I be held responsible? It wasn't my fault that I have this "random release of neurotransmitters in my brain" condition.

30 My attorney would argue the point that my will wasn't free since it was due to a "random release of neurotransmitters in my brain" and there was nothing I could do to stop it from happening.

31 For pragmatic and reasons of utility (usefulness), I would be separated from society because I would be a danger to "myself or others." But fundamentally (in the eyes of The Lord God and hopefully the progressive newspapers of tomorrow), I am still fundamentally innocent.

The progressive papers of tomorrow will say: "You can still fear someone, but you just can't hate them. This person is blamelessly responsible."

32 Imagine what your life would be like if all your actions, intentions, desires, and beliefs, were "self-generated" or first caused in this random way: you would scarcely seem to have a mind at all.

33 Your life would be totally and utterly rudderless. You would be beyond lost and unable to make any decision at all since they would all seem equally good to you. You wouldn't learn from your mistakes and your decision making would be complete madness.

With "free will" all choices would look exactly equal. You would no longer have any preferences. How would you know what to do next? The answer is you wouldn't. "Free Will" causes complete madness. It is only because we don't have free will that anything gets done at all (just the opposite of what most people think).

34 Actions, intentions, beliefs, and desires can only exist in a system that is significantly constrained by patterns of behavior and the laws of stimulus-response (law of causation).

35 How is it that we can communicate with other human beings? How is it that you can read what I am writing?

36 To find my teachings and writings comprehensible at all one needs to recognize patterns and draw on past experiences of what something means. What if I wrote "jf kw f=wfsf k;slkkdjf hen knd nn—d=o=e\e\\." Would you know what that meant?

37 To communicate at all means the law of causation: It all depends on the assumption that my thoughts when written will obediently conform to a shared reality (that being more or less correct English grammar we all learned in school). So in this perspective, Heisenberg's "self-generated" mental events would amount to utter ramblings of an incoherent author who next sentence would look something like this: eohjrewjfhsdjh; js;kldnw, =-\\w\w) (* *(8-9&*()&*04i oko;k;lsgkndgi0-8-I80*(0-i9=9 kflsk psd=\=\\p\\p-\?;klk"

38 To see that the addition of randomness -- quantum mechanical or otherwise -- does nothing to change the situation that our wills are not free and our lives are not up to us.

39 The law of causation makes it possible for you to read this sentence and understand what the "law of causation" even means. There is a cause to you understanding how to read English and a cause for me on how to write a teaching in English. If the law of randomness not causation ruled the universe the next sentence would be ksakjf ksjf;' j[-23]=2r=2-r\204iir 40-ri 2i0r.

40 Do subatomic particles have free will? I think not. Neither Quantum Mechanics nor such things as The Heisenberg Uncertainty Principle salvage free will and to imply otherwise is simply incorrect.

The Holy Bible: No Free Will. Amen.

Book Eight by The Conditioner

The Book of
Everything Conditions You

Chapter One

"Because of the illusion of free will (the law of causation), Heaven and Hell either don't exist or people are predetermined to go to either one. God cannot judge a man or woman without a free will. It's total, complete, utter insanity and nonsense to believe in free will. It's the biggest fairy tale out there."

—Nick Vale

Here's a look at the two major conditioning models.

Classical Conditioning

The typical procedure for inducing classical conditioning involves presentations of a neutral stimulus along with a stimulus of some significance, the "unconditional stimulus." The neutral stimulus could be any event that does not result in an overt behavioral response from the organism under investigation. Conversely, presentation of the significant stimulus necessarily evokes an innate, often reflexive, response. Pavlov called these the unconditional stimulus (US) and unconditional response (UR), respectively.

2. If the neutral stimulus is presented along with the unconditional stimulus, it would become a conditional stimulus (CS). Pavlov used the term conditional because he wanted to emphasize that learning required a dependent or conditional relationship between CS and US. If the CS and US always occur together and never alone, this perfect dependent relationship or pairing, causes the two stimuli to become associated and the organism produces a behavioral response to the CS. Pavlov called this the conditional response (CR).
3. Operant Conditioning

Classical conditioning forms an association between two stimuli. Operant conditioning forms an association between a behavior and a consequence. This is what so people refer to as "carrots or sticks conditioning. Carrots are rewards and sticks are the punishments. It is also called response-stimulus or RS conditioning because it forms an association between the animal's response [behavior] and the stimulus that follows [consequence].)

Four Possible Consequences

There are four possible consequences to any behavior. They are the following:

> **Something good can start or be presented;
> something good can end or be taken away;
> something bad can start or be presented;
> something bad can end or be taken away.**

4. Consequences have to be immediate or clearly linked to the behavior. With verbal humans, we can explain the connection between the consequence and the behavior even if they are separated in time.
5. For example, you might tell a friend that you'll buy dinner for them since they helped you move, or a parent might explain that

the child can't go to summer camp because of her bad grades. With very young children, humans who don't have verbal skills, and animals, you can't explain the connection between the consequence and the behavior. For the animal, the consequence has to be immediate. The way to work around this is to use a bridge (see above).

6 Technical Terms

The technical term for "an event started" or "an item presented" is positive since it's something that's added to the animal's environment.

The technical term for "an event ended" or "an item taken away" is negative since it's something that's subtracted from the animal's environment.

7. Anything that increases a behavior -- makes it occur more frequently, makes it stronger, or makes it more likely to occur -- is termed a reinforcer. Often, an animal (or person) will perceive "starting something good" or "ending something bad" as something worth pursuing, and they will repeat the behaviors that seem to cause these consequences.

8. These consequences will increase the behaviors that lead to them; they are reinforcers. These are consequences the animal will work to attain, so they strengthen the behavior.

9. Anything that decreases a behavior -- makes it occur less frequently, makes it weaker, or makes it less likely to occur -- is termed a punisher. Often, an animal (or person) will perceive "ending something good" or "starting something bad" as something worth avoiding, and they will not repeat the behaviors that seem to cause these consequences. These consequences will decrease the behaviors that lead to them; they are punishers.

10. Applying these terms to the four possible consequences, you get this:

Something good can start or be presented, so behavior increases = Positive Reinforcement (R+)

Something good can end or be taken away, so behavior decreases = Negative Punishment (P-)

Something bad can start or be presented, so behavior decreases = Positive Punishment (P+)

Something bad can end or be taken away, so behavior increases = Negative Reinforcement (R-)

Or

	Reinforcement (behavior increases)	Punishment (behavior decreases)
Positive (something added)	Positive Reinforcement Something added increases behavior.	Positive Punishment Something added decreases behavior.
Negative (something removed)	Negative Reinforcement Something removed increases behavior.	Negative Punishment Something removed decreases behavior.

11 Remember that these definitions are based on their actual effect on the behavior in question: they must reduce or strengthen the behavior to be considered a consequence and be defined as a punishment or reinforcement.
12 Pleasures meant as rewards but that do not strengthen a behavior are indulgences, not reinforcement; aversives meant as a behavior weakener but which do not weaken a behavior are abuse, not punishment. Either way, one thing always leads to another by simply conditioning the various human energy systems any way you slice it.
13 So in a nutshell everything in life is constantly conditioning you one way or another. Described above are the two main conditioning models that happen to us while we are on earth. Don't forget the culture in which you live. The culture conditions

you as well. It is not a "direct conditioning model" but rather a more subtle and indirect overall "conditioning model."

14 Remember as kids when you and I played baseball or softball for the very first time we ran on contact from first base to second base even though the outfielder had caught the ball. Remember how we learned that made an out. That pain we felt for making a silly out. But if no one had previously properly explained the rule to us how were we to know? We weren't born knowing that rule. Then we learned we could "tag up" and run to the next base but only after the ball was caught.

15 The prior pain of making an out on this play had conditioned us to learn from our previous base running blunder (mistake). That's how we learn things and get conditioned responses. The next time we were on first base and the ball was hit to the outfield, we then waited on the bag to make sure it wasn't caught before we began running to second base. Then we either "tagged up" or didn't—another learned (conditioned) response. Same external event, different response due to conditioning.

16 Conditioned responses and reflexive or instinctual (innate) responses make us the human beings we are today. Free will is nowhere to be found.

"Everyone in this town is conservative and married. That's just how it is here."

—The Conditioner

"That's how we've been doing it for thousands of years. It's just how we do things here. We'll pick out a good wife for you, don't worry."

—The Conditioner

The Holy Bible: No Free Will. Amen.

Book Nine by The Conduit

The Book of

Paradigm Shift

Chapter One

"New truth is often uncomfortable. Especially to the holders of power the new truth threatens."

—The Conduit

Question: What is a paradigm shift?

Answer: A paradigm shift occurs basically when an old theory becomes creaky or leaky, and people start to feel or notice that the viewpoint expounded by the theory no longer makes much sense anymore as new information comes to light. The new information has to be explained in a way so that it fits a new theory, thereby making the old theory outdated or obsolete. Basically, the new theory simply makes more sense, and people can feel it deep in their bones, period.

2   The science and philosophy of free will lacks a solid paradigm; that is for sure. How come people can't just choose to get out of their depressions? Why can't we just choose to be happy? If we had a free will, why wouldn't we just choose happy thoughts all of the time?

"If I had a free will I would never be depressed. I would simply always choose to be happy. I would always choose to do good and always choose to be a perfect angel. Nobody would get divorced because nobody would ever fall out of love."

—The Conduit

"What total, complete, utter insanity and nonsense the belief in free will is."

—The Conduit

The Holy Bible: No Free Will. Amen.

Book Ten by The Custodian

The Book of

Myth Of Free Will

Chapter One

FREE will is said to be the most debated philosophical problem ever. It is normally left for philosophers to debate and it gets lost in academia. It is now time for this problem to be brought to the center of Main Street on Truth Ave.

2. It concerns all of us all the time because it reeks with issues of morality, responsibility, criminal punishment, reward systems, day to day living, thoughts of revenge, thoughts of hate and blame, intelligence, overall life, wisdom, truth, and how lives are lead in reality.
3. The belief in free will is the belief that every person is the true first cause or source of his or her thoughts and actions. It concerns everything we do. From personal achievement or failure, law, politics, religion, public policy, romantic relationships, feelings of guilt and remorse, and well just about everything we have ever done or said, it is at first difficult to believe that free will is just an illusion.

4   The facts are the facts and the facts are cause and effect reign supreme in the universe and all human lives.
5   Why not live our human lives according to truth instead of living in an illusion? Why not have a public debate about the issue? Why is this topic still in hiding? Why has every other "taboo" subject made its way into the main stream except this one?
6   Why are vibrators being advertised on television, gay marriage is being discussed openly, suicide finally out in the open, pornography on regular television twenty four hours a day with a click of the button, free internet hardcore porn that a six year old can easily download, money, sex, religion, and politics openly talked about, and erectile dysfunction ads on during prime time . . . yet no one (as of yet and that's about to change) wants to discuss publicly the most important topic of the entire history of our species?
7   The topic of "free will" will be the most important "taboo" subject matter ever discussed and debated in the history of time (when it finally comes out of hiding). Enough with academia and philosophy class already. Let's bring this topic to the people.

"It is now time for the debate on whether or not humans have a free will to be brought to the center of Main Street on Truth Ave. We the people want to know the truth and we want to be on CNN live during prime time. Let the people know the truth about their wills. Let them hear both sides of the story."

—The Custodian

8   The illusion of free will is so prevalent in our society that many people don't even know they are living all these years in a lie. This is the Mythical Monster of the times we live in.
9   It's been said that this Myth (the myth of free will) is so prevalent it would be like asking the fish in the sea how the water is. In other words, it is all around us all the time and that causes us (the vast majority of human beings, not me of course) do not even be aware that it is there. It's simply taken as truth like the

air we breathe. It is the faultiest of faulty assumptions to say the very least.

10 Free will is a faulty assumption to say the least. The truth of the matter is this: The most fundamental aspect of being a human being is to understand that our wills are not free. We've got it all wrong and it is now time to live our lives according to truth instead of living in an illusion.

"If free will existed, why wouldn't we all just simply choose to do good all of the time? Why would we choose depression and suicide? Why not just choose to be happy?"

—The Custodian

"You have nothing to lose in reading this section of the book because what you're about to lose you never had in the first place (your sense of "free" will). Amen."

—The Custodian

11 People *have the feeling of free will*. It's just a feeling. Feelings are not facts. How many people feel as if they are something they are not? If I felt I were a God would that make me a God?
12 Just like *the feeling* something is real during a magic trick. Just because you *feel like* something is true doesn't make it true. I used *to feel* Santa Claus was a real person. I also felt that way about the Easter Bunny, the Sandman and the Tooth Fairy.
13 The soul or spirit inside issue:

Our lives are conditioned. If there is a soul or spirit wouldn't it too learn from its mistakes and have a causally chained trajectory? Why would a spirit or soul be a so—called first causer over and over again with no constraints, determinants, or memories to fall back or learn from?

14 Why would a soul or spirit not also be subject to classical and operant conditioning (or any other type of conditioning that exists?).

15 If your soul or spirit is giving you that magical feeling of "free will" what exactly is it basing its decision making process on?
16 It makes much more sense to believe your soul or spirit gets conditioned from the moment we are conceived.

"If my soul or spirit were making decisions for me, how would that mean I would have a free will? The exact opposite would actually be true as I'd feel more out of control than ever."

—The Custodian

17 Advantages to not having a free will include a whole new mentality that will serve as the new underpinnings of our humanity and our human being experience. For example: Anything that happens in life "could've just as easily been me" mentality will begin to be taught in schools thereby fostering its growth. This will foster a much more compassionate attitude towards our fellow man. Free Will has been correlated to more homicides (see book by The Harmer, book nineteen).
18 Question: If free will is in fact a myth, we can then conclude that judgment of our human life would be impossible by an all knowing God. So if there is no judgment made of our human life you may be wondering the following . . . why would people try to do good or even be polite to one another?
19 Answer: Evolutionary survival psychology provides reasons why we want to be good and polite towards our fellow man (even though there will be no judgment day forthcoming).
20 First we have our genetics which causes us to have such things as nurturing instincts most exemplified by kin favoritism. Then we have the fact that being good and polite helps us to survive due to the fact it is always a good idea to earn brownie points in the game of reciprocal altruism.
21 For example think of living in a small town on the prairie and your neighbor asks you if he or she can borrow some sugar. If you say no, then one day when you are out of sugar, the odds that they will then lend you sugar is significantly decreased (why should I? He didn't lend it to me in my time of need mentality will win out).

22. It is better to be nice to one's neighbors because what comes around goes around just makes surviving easier and more likely. Karma dictates that what comes around goes around so being polite and nice to one another will never go away (even without free will—so don't worry about that).
23. Question: If free will doesn't exist—how do I actually do anything? Why don't we all just stay in bed all day and lie around and do absolutely nothing?
24. Answer: Assuming you had the money to live such a lifestyle this is how your day would most likely unfold: First you would wake up and just lay there for hours and hours and eventually get bored.
25. Then you would have to go to the bathroom. Once in the bathroom it seems nicer to have a shower and brush ones teeth than not so you'd probably do that too.
26. Then you would want to go back to bed, but you would notice that you felt hungry and feel it's better to get something to eat than not. And so the day goes on and things get done.
27. In fact, if you keep practicing this way it becomes increasingly obvious that the physical body you once thought you had complete control over, does not need your "free will" decision making powers after all. It does just fine on its own thank you very much.
28. What appears to be controlling our bodies is in fact a lifetime of instinctual and learned conditioned responses (conscious, unconscious, and subconscious) distributed to us through its multiple parallel acting systems such as instincts, memories, control systems, and skills of a lifetime that will ensure (for survival reasons) that the human body learns appropriate and then optimal responses to every situation it has ever been in or could be in.

"There are only two types of people in the world. Those who believe in free will and those who do not. There is no such thing as a little free will. There is no wiggle room here. It's a black or white issue."

—The Custodian

29. As stated previously, if we do in fact have a soul or a spirit, it's safe to say, it gets conditioned as well.

"One must always remember the simple fact of causality. Every moment of the universe is dependent on the moment before. Human lives are no different. Human lives are obviously in the universe and not outside it."

—The Custodian

The Holy Bible: No Free Will. Amen.

Chapter Two

EACH of us lives in a difficult to predict present and near future, which includes our own behavior in it, and which therefore makes our behavior feel spontaneous and undetermined/uncaused—but what we don't experience, yet which are just as real, are the multitude of un/subconscious influences and determinants of what we think, act, and feel (from our past).

2. Many people argue with me and say "I have free will because it feels like I have it." I tell them -- "just because you feel or believe you have or are something does that make it true? If you feel or believe you're right about something are you always proven correct? Haven't you ever felt something to be true yet it wasn't?" Just ask anyone who has ever been in a romantic relationship and "felt" it was "true love" but it didn't work out. Feelings are not facts. Plain and simple.
3. We often believe that if we wish hard enough for something it will come true. We twist and distort the facts to fit what feels best to us on the inside. We rationalize everything to make ourselves feel better. If it feels better internally to believe in the nonsensical belief in free will then that is what we will end up believing in.
4. On the other hand if it feels best for us internally to believe that free will is a myth and an illusion then that is what we will end up believing. Somehow—I believe the truth will inevitably make us feel better (once we understand it).

"Most, if not all people prefer truth to illusion. They just need the truth properly explained to them."

—The Custodian

"Copernicus, Galileo, and Columbus are all examples of how the truth wins out once the facts are made crystal clear. I don't see why free will being an illusion will be any different."

—The Custodian

5   So why does the truth matter?

Because our survival in this high tech world depends on our being honest with ourselves, on understanding who we really are, as our true nature. In primitive societies, illusions and pseudoscience had benefits. Today is different and the people know it.

6   They can feel it, and they can sense it. Evolution of consciousness is the next step for mankind as we become more and more aware of the truth of how human lives are lead in reality. It's as if we are at the same magic show getting tricked over and over again by the same exact illusion.
7   At some point, the collective consciousness (aka "The People") are going to say "enough with that trick already—we are sick of it! We've seen it a million times already and it just doesn't trick us anymore." Let's move on now because we are now ready for some truth.
8   Illusions at a magic show can be fun for a while, but sooner or later, the smoke and mirrors stuff just becomes tiresome. The Illusion of Free Will is now tiresome. It's worn out. The time has come to put it to rest.

The Holy Bible: No Free Will. Amen.

Chapter Three

UNDERSTANDING that free will is pure illusion and total, complete, utter insanity and nonsense gets rid of a lot of negative consequences. Instead of extreme and severe blame, regret, resentment, revenge, envy, and an escalating culture of an "eye for an eye" mentality which is a never ending sequence of violence and hatred (for example as described in Elliot Rodger's My Twisted World manifesto), people will instead blame the universe or the entire cosmos for their misfortune (not themselves or other people) or even better just accept "it is what it is, it's my fate." You can still be pragmatically upset at someone of course, but you will also know concurrently that fundamentally they simply couldn't help themselves (even if they have hurt you terribly). People will understand the difference between severe and extreme emotional blame and practical, logistical, or pragmatic blame. People will also understand the idea of "blameless or faultless responsibility." People now knowing that free will is one big lie, will still feel pragmatic guilt (we need that to correct mistakes we've made), but future humanity will be spared life threatening and life piercing deep personal shame or embarrassment (caused by the belief that we and others have free will and could have done otherwise).

> 2 Severe emotional blame (with free will) makes you hate someone so much you want to kill them. Practical or pragmatic blame (no free will) allows you to "pragmatically blame" them and sue them (to get what you feel is fair in the situation at hand), but without the severe internal emotional turmoil that eats you up inside when you fundamentally (truly) blame yourself or someone else. You will always remember the difference between the pragmatic and the fundamental (true) nature of people and things. The true nature of human beings is that they do not have free will.

A) People who believe in "free will" surely practice "blameful responsibility" and want to see the other person severely punished. They want revenge and retribution. They want to see others punished to the point of severe suffering. This causes an escalating cycle of hatred in mankind (think Elliot Rodger).

B) People who know "free will" is an illusion will practice "blameless or faultless responsibility." They want admonishment, deterrence, rehabilitation, restraint and/or removal (for safety reasons and rightly so). They want to see others "learn their lesson" as to make sure it will never happen again. They want to see others reconditioned and able to rejoin society. They want punishment only for deterrence purposes and not for revenge or retribution.

Which way do you think will create a better society—A or B?

Why did you choose what you did?

3. What was the cause of your decision?

"You technically can't blame the universe either for its will is also causally chained, but it's sure a lot better than blaming fallible people. The universe is a cause and effect robotic monster of epic proportions."

—The Custodian

4. How can the discovery that "free will" is total, complete, utter insanity and nonsense help us? What are the benefits and how can it make us all feel better?
5. When someone behaves badly, or even violently, or more to the point heinously lying like a Bernie Madoff situation, the son (Mark) would probably still feel pragmatic shame, but not to the point (severe emotional and fundamental shame) that he would end up committing suicide.
6. He would've been able to simply tell himself "my father simply couldn't have acted any other way. He had conditioned himself to get away with it and there was no turning back to his unchecked greed. He did not have a free will. It was all fated to be that way." If Mark Madoff did not attribute free will to his father (or himself for that matter) I'm sure he'd be alive today.
7. The same would be true for that Chicago Cubs fan in 2003 who instinctively interfered with a catchable ball that cost his team a crucial out. In the future, when people are raised, taught,

and learn that they don't have free will, a more compassionate society will then foster and grow.

8. Therefore, when a situation arises like The Cubs fan, instead of the emotional reaction of pelting him with beer and obscenities and making the poor fellow go into hiding, people will always know deep down that it was just fate causing him to play the role as the scapegoat.

9. Each fan would be more compassionate because they would also know deep down that it could have just as easily been them sitting in that chair reaching for that ball.

10. The entire way we view reality will change once we understand that free will doesn't exist.

11. Understanding the difference between severe emotional blame (free will based society) and pragmatic blame (unfree will based society) will signify the beginning of the long awaited evolution of human consciousness.

12. Same is true for understanding the difference between "blameful responsibility" (free will based mindset) and "blameless or faultless responsibility" (no free will based mindset).

13. Understanding something called * "the universe compelled pragmatic pursuits of perceived fair exchanges of human energy" will then be the next domino to fall in the great crumbling of the "delusional free will age" that we currently live in.

14. The same would be true for so called "villains" and "heroes." Instead of a society that over demonizes their "villains" and over decorates and idolizes their "heroes," we would become a society that would understand that the individual in question was simply exhibiting his past experiences and genetics (nature and nurture).

15. I'm not saying there aren't "good" guys and "bad" guys. All I am saying is that these people you call good or evil were just fated to be so. They did not freely will it upon themselves and that really needs to be understood better by a society seeking truth.

16. In fact every time I hear a so called "hero" interviewed on television, the so called "hero" does not feel they did something heroic. They claim they did "what anyone would do in that situation." They feel lucky that people consider them a hero. In a

---

* learn this concept in my book "Enlightenment Through Entitlement"

no free will based society people will either consider themselves lucky or unlucky or somewhere in between on this spectrum.
17 People will still feel slightly praiseworthy and slightly blameworthy (for practical and pragmatic reasons) but not to the degree we currently hold so dear to us as the fabric maintaining our entire society (emotional reasons).
18 On a larger "free will" based insanity scale: Nations, religions, and groups of people cast severe emotional blame onto one another all the time. Wars, leading to further wars which, in turn, lead to more demonstrate that there has been very little to no progress in the understanding or acceptance of the concept that free will is total illusion and total utter nonsense. This new kind of Holy Bible: No Free Will aims to change that.
19 The Illusion of Free Will is a very bad and dangerous habit and an extremely hard one to break (kind of like smoking). For example: when a nation, religion, or a people decide that another nation, religion, or a people has a set of values that they don't agree with or like, the pervasive attitude is that it is much easier to bomb someone else's house (and assume they have free will) than to clean up one's own home (and get the illusion of free will thing right once and for all) on "your side of the street."
20 The word Hero or Heroes is great for marketing purposes:

For example: Heroes tend to "sacrifice." In reality there is no such thing as sacrifice. A better word for sacrifice is investment.

21 In fundamental reality—there are fundamentally no such things as heroes, sacrifices, martyrs, villains, and saints. Without free will—people are fundamentally neither praiseworthy nor blameworthy. In practical, logistical, conventional, useful, pragmatic reality there are in fact heroes and villains and everything in between.
22 Here are some examples in practical reality:

Yes you "sacrifice" for your children and spouse for selfish reasons (which may or may not make them and you happy). Yes you "sacrifice" for your country or parents (which may or may not make them and you happy). Yes you may martyr yourself for your country or cause (which may or may not make them and you happy). Yes you may do "altruistic" charity work (which may or may not make them and you happy).

23 These are all examples of methods of how people attempt to make themselves happy, content, or just plain satisfied first and foremost. Now, none of these examples, of course, really involves sacrifice, martyrdom, or altruism at all. What is really involved at its most basic and fundamental level is selfishness and personal investment for a better life somewhere down the road (delayed gratification).

24 The person who is doing all this "sacrificing, martyring, and altruism" is really acting on the conditioned or instinctual belief that the good they hope to receive back from their efforts will be worth their time, energy, effort, money etc., in exchange for such things as G-d's good favor, good afterlife, having people like them, having people think they are a "good person" etc. They are not sacrificing. They are in reality investing (for a better after life for example).

25 People whether they admit it or not want a [1] "perceived fair exchange of their human energy" that they had expended in the doing of all their good deeds for the other person(s) or cause(s). They want a return on their investment (time, effort, and energy).

26 What about the person who risks his life to save another person? On a *pragmatic/superficial level this person is in fact a hero. But on the deeper and truer/fundamental level this person is fundamentally doing this:

This person risked his life for another because he was acting on the belief that risking one's life in trying to rescue the other person will make this person feel better knowing he tried to save the other person than live the rest of his life with the thought that another human being died whom he might have been otherwise been able to save.

27 To clarify above: What is the difference between "fundamentally and pragmatically?" Fundamentally means in the eyes of the Almighty/Creator. It is the deepest and truest nature of something. This is also known in some circles as the

---

[1] learn this concept in my book "Enlightenment Through Entitlement"
* Pragmatically means in the eyes of human beings.

"absolute" or "the divine." Pragmatically means in the eyes of human beings. It is on the most practical and superficial level of what is most useful. *See another example of the pragmatic level at the end of this chapter.

28 My advice to people who aren't sure if they have free will or not is this: Read this book and any other book you can find on the topic that argues against mankind having a free will.
29 Simply google the topic and buy the books. Then do the same for the books that argue that man does in fact possess a free will. Then lose interest in the topic or not (it's all fated anyway how much interest you have in this topic in the first place).
30 Simply hear both sides of the story and then decide whether you believe you have it or not. To be fair to yourself and to the topic at hand, don't you believe you owe it to yourself to give equal time, effort, and energy to both sides?
31 Here's how you can quickly and easily refute anyone arguing with you about having a free will:

- Ask the free will believer to give an example of a choice that they believe to have been freely chosen.
- Wait for their answer. Now ask the free will believer to say whether or not the choice was caused (what their reason was for the choice they made).
- Congratulations. You have just won the argument that everything has to have a cause.

The Holy Bible: No Free Will. Amen.

* Defendant says "I had no choice your honor."

Judge says "I also have no choice. For pragmatic reasons I have no choice but to keep society safe and you now need to be removed and reconditioned so that you will no longer make society unsafe."

Chapter Four

THINK about this for a second. If we had a free will, why wouldn't we always simply choose to do good? Why would any evil happen at all? Given the free choice don't you think all humans would prefer to only do only good?

Any crime, however heinous, is in principle the visible manifestation of someone's antecedent conditions acting through the accused physiology, heredity, and environment.

2. Personal "blameless/faultless responsibility" will still exist (pragmatically speaking), it's just that ultimate (true) responsibility will no longer exist (fundamentally/truly speaking). Ultimate in this context means whether or not one goes to heaven or hell for the rest of eternity.
3. We must learn to understand the universe compelled pragmatic pursuits of* perceived fair exchanges of human energy (another way of saying nature's justice system).
4. In other words, humans will one day say to one another "the universe is not on my side or fate has dealt me a terrible situation here. I feel very unlucky because of this situation. I desire to feel lucky again. I must correct it and I have no choice in the matter but to get what I feel is fair. In short, I have no choice but to pragmatically sue you because I do not feel what has transpired between us was just and fair."
5. In short, from a practical human perspective there is fated good and evil. From the Universe's/Cosmos'/Almighty Creator's/ Higher Power's perspective (whatever you want to call it), there can be, never was, and never will be any judgment for our human lives for we have fundamentally and truly not willed them freely.
6. Likewise, if everything is just random, then we are also in a similar situation as stated above. How can we be held ultimately and (truly) fundamentally accountable for our actions if everything is simply random?

---

* learn this concept in my book "Enlightenment Through Entitlement"

7   Never judge a human until you have walked and were born into his exact same shoes (karmic stream of fate), atom for atom, and quark for quark. Same mind and same soul etc.
8   So just because everything is predetermined and fated does that mean all of life is a waste of time?
9   Have you ever read a good mystery novel or rented a movie? The real reason we go to the movies or read a novel is to watch and experience how well the movie/novel is made and the way the story unfolds with all of its surprising twists and turns.
10 It's from the amazement and awe of how the story unfolds that our pleasure is derived. Why read a book in the first place? Why not just skip to the last chapter? Why watch a DVD movie at home at all? Why not just skip to the last scene and see how it all turns out?
11 Life (without a free will) is still all about the journey, not the destination.
12 Understanding that the decisions we make are the result of our prior determinants, prior causes, and our prior reasons, provides a perspective on life that is amazing, elegant, and most importantly truthful. Just as every moment in the universe is dependent on the moment before, so do our everyday actions reflect this continuity of cause and effect. We are inside the universe, not outside of it. The universe operates by cause and effect. The universe is deterministic through and through and will one day be proved to be so scientifically. It can be no other way. Quantum Mechanics will one day reflect this truth as it is safe to assume every hidden variable has yet to be discovered. We just discovered the Higgs Boson in 2012 and the last quark a mere 27 years ago. Not to mention the new discovery of exotic particles in 2022 which include the pentaquark and the tetraquark.
13 Gerard 't Hooft (Nobel Prize in Physics 1999) also firmly believes that there should be a deterministic theory underlying quantum mechanics.
14 The incorrect belief in free will is so pervasive in our society it would be like asking the fish how the water is. They don't even know they live in water. They just do and that's all they know. Quite simply we are bombarded with the assumption that man has free will every day, everywhere, all the time.

15 I'm actually amazed that a small minority of people don't believe in the nonsense of free will. It's actually a miracle that these people exist.
16 If you would like to help this cause, please start a no free will or exploring the illusion of free will meet-up group in your hometown or city. Thank you.
17 Help spread the word that man's will is not free.

The Holy Bible: No Free Will. Amen.

Chapter Five

"Our parents gave birth to us. We did not self - create ourselves. We did not choose our parents or how we were raised."

—The Custodian

What about a last second decision or a last second changing of the mind?

Like every other moment in time, the moment immediately preceding our decision to change our mind is connected to every prior decision we have ever made. That new decision still reflects the entire history of our genes and the way they have interacted with our environment. This is how we become the people we are today.

"Human beings desire this and that because of a cause (conditioned response) or many causes (conditioned responses) that are determined by other prior causes (conditioned responses). This realization teaches us to fundamentally blame no one, resent no one, blame no one, to be jealous of no one, and to forgive everyone."

"Everything is either causal or random. Neither proves 'free' will."

"You are a product of your genetics and your conditioned learned responses (life experiences). Free will is nowhere to be found."

—The Custodian

> 2 Free Will is an illusion, but it's a very persistent illusion -- it keeps coming back at us like a boomerang. Even though you now know it's a trick, if you don't keep your awareness guard up, you'll be likely to get fooled time and time again.

Why are you reading this book? Why are you reading a book called The Holy Bible: No Free Will? And what is the cause of that?

"Everything has to have a cause or a reason. It doesn't matter if you consciously know the cause or reason."

—The Custodian

3. A team of scientific psychologists could one day in theory study every reported thought, emotion, motive, gene, decision, effect of that decision, your history of learning and conditioning, memories, culture, physiology, microanatomy, nueroanatomy and lots of other things.
4. If it were possible to have access to all the data and variables they could ever want, they could uncover the mechanism (like a machine, robot, or calibrated clock) that gave rise to all your behavior and so could explain why you picked up a book called The Holy Bible: No Free Will at this particular moment in time.
5. It's 100% unlikely that you simply freely willed to pick up this book and began reading it without any prior causes. If you truly believe that your desire to read this book was a freely willed desire, then you would be the first causer and be God. Are you God? I think not.
6. Everything comes from that first cause (the big bang for example) or infinity (no first cause). If infinity then cause and effect have been with us forever and ever.
7. What would it be like to be a first causer and have free will? For starters, we would be able to sidestep our brain's prior programming and be able to act and think without being influenced by our genes and conditioning.
8. Why isn't my behavior predictable you may be asking yourself if all that is written here is true?
9. The answer is that so much of our programming is unconscious/subconscious and the variables too many to number to know consciously why we do what we do at any moment in time.
10. Many people believe they have free will because they are conscious of their thought processes leading up to a carefully made decision (the tip of the iceberg).
11. What they don't know is what is in the iceberg. Therefore it is safe to say that people are unconscious of the subconscious causes by which all of their decision making is determined.

12 Sometimes, many causes contribute to a single effect or many effects may result from a single cause. The realization that our behavior is produced by un/subconscious and conscious causes enables us to believe that free will is a belief of the past.

"There was the Ice Age, The Stone Age, The Dark Ages, and The Industrial Revolution. In the future, historians will look back at this time period as The Nonsensical Free Will Age."

"The point of this new kind of Holy Bible is not to figure out how the universe was created. That will most likely never happen so there is no point in trying. The point of the book is to refute free will."

—Nick Vale

13 Some simple examples of cause and effect:

Cause: It starts to rain

Effect: You buy an umbrella

Cause: There's an earthquake

Effect: You start to run

Cause: You feel like you're getting a burn in the sun

Effect: You buy sunscreen and apply it or simply find shade

The Holy Bible: No Free Will. Amen.

Book Eleven by The Gifter

The Book of

The Greatest Gift

Chapter One

"We almost always (if not always) pursue what we perceive to be right and fair. If it means we must pragmatically sue someone then that is what we must do. Now that we all know that free will is pure illusion we just can't fundamentally blame people and banish their souls to an eternity burning in hell or put devil's horns on them with a red coat and a pitch fork. Actions will always have pragmatic consequences, but will also always have fundamental innocence."

—The Gifter

"Blame the situation (or the entirety of the universe), not the other person."

—The Gifter

"People don't like to take responsibility for their actions because deep down and fundamentally there was no other choice in the situation. People are always doing the very best they can."

—The Gifter

2. To be clear, everything in life is a value for value exchange or otherwise known as a *perceived fair exchange of human time, effort, and energy (money is a form of energy). Due to the optimization, hedonic, and fairness imperatives, we humans have no choice but to maximize and optimize every second of our life so that we can shield ourselves from the terrible emotion of regret and "if only I had done this and that differently." So we have no choice but to always be doing the best we can (at the time!). Sometimes, if doing the "best we can at the time" means staying in bed all day then so be it. It may seem to others on the outside that we are being lazy, but due to all the invisible pressures, stressors, and causes we feel, sometimes we simply cannot get out of bed.

"If you could have acted otherwise, you would have."

"If you could have acted otherwise, why didn't you?"

—The Gifter

3. Just staying alive sometimes is "doing the best we can at that particular moment in time." Our bodies for all sorts of emotional and physical reasons simply cannot muster up the strength to get out of bed and do well anything. When we stay in bed all day and night, very little human energy is expended and then very little human energy will be expected in.

---

* learn this concept in my book "Enlightenment Through Entitlement"

4   There is always a value for value * "perceived fair exchange of human energy" being transferred amongst people and things (sometimes it's a short term thing and other times it's a long term exchange). It is not an exact science and is not calculated mathematically obviously. It's most definitely a rough and nebulous kind of calculation stored in one's body over a period of time. It is simply the invisible world of reality that is taking place.

"Once you realize that your decisions were all predetermined, and that you had no choice but to make them, you can immediately forgive yourself for all the silly and stupid mistakes that you made. I'm The Gifter and that is the greatest gift of all."

—The Gifter

5   The other great gift in life is that since we do not have a free will we cannot fundamentally rank destinies. For practical reasons we like to, but fundamentally (truly) and ultimately we cannot. We cannot compare our lives to others and rank or judge who has a superior or better life (thanks to no free will).
6   "Compare and despair" as they say.
7   The Messiah is not a person. The Messiah is the natural law that man's will is not free. By understanding that man's will is not free, people will in fact be saved from many highly toxic and self-destructive thoughts and behaviors.

"Believing in free will is totally, completely, and utterly nonsensical (not to mention insane). It is also a royal pain in the ass. Once you give up your belief in free will, you will release the heavy burden of comparing yourself to others. Who needs a belief that causes so much stress and agitation?"

—The Gifter

8   This is because once we realize our karmic trajectories were not chosen freely by us, we have no choice but to not "compare and despair." How can we be upset with ourselves for not attaining

---

* learn this concept in my book "Enlightenment Through Entitlement"

or accomplishing more with our lives when our karmic streams were predetermined to begin with?

9 Nothing is fundamentally our fault or our accomplishment -- so now we can no longer rank human destinies. This gift is the realization that jealousy is an emotion based on humans having free wills. Since that premise is false, then jealousy is fundamentally a "false" emotion or an emotion based on an illusion.

"Other people accomplish things just because they, not you, were fated to do so. The universe compels you to do what you do and the same is true for everyone else. No one is acting with free will, so that should free you of jealousy and destiny ranking since no one had, has, or will have a choice in the matter of anything."

—The Gifter

"I was simply fated to write this book and you were not."

—Nick Vale

10 Deep down we know that we are always doing the best we can in any circumstance even though it may not appear that way to others. This is yet another reason that makes free will impossible. If we are always doing the very best we can then everything had to turn out exactly the way it did (and will). Everything can therefore be considered God's will.

11 Deep down we know that we couldn't have done otherwise in every single situation we were ever in and will ever be in. Elliot Rodger knew he was twisted. That's why he called his manifesto "My Twisted World." Therefore, this proves humans do not have free will. Why would someone who knew he was twisted not untwist himself? Surely step one is acknowledgement. The truth is he was just a witness to his life. We all are. If he had free will, surely he would have untwisted his "twisted world." He could not do otherwise because his will was not free. This is the one gift he left behind. He clearly showed in his detailed manifesto how man's will is not free. He even said he didn't

want things to turn out this way. I think Elliot would have felt a whole lot better if he knew his will (and the will of others) was not free.
12 So if we can constantly remind ourselves that our wills are not free, then destiny ranking, self—blame, self - hatred, and all the mistakes we made in the past and will be made in the future can all be easily forgiven.

"The greatest gift of all is the gift of unconditionally accepting yourself. The best was to achieve this goal is to understand man's will is not free."

—The Gifter

"What a relief to know that I can say goodbye to all the silly mistakes I made in life. All I had to do was understand the illusion of free will. Once this understanding was internalized, I immediately forgave myself for everything that I felt I had done wrong in my life. I now know that I was always doing the best I could at the time and that everything was and will be predetermined."

—The Gifter

13 Say this to yourself every time you get upset about a mistake you made:

"I had no choice. There was nothing else I could have done **at that time**. *I did what I felt was the right thing to do* **at the time**. *I cannot just will whatever I want whenever I want."*

—The Gifter

"You did the best you could at the time."

—The Gifter

The Holy Bible: No Free Will. Amen.

Book Twelve by The Reality Teller

The Book of

It Is What It Is

Chapter One

"You can still fear people. You just can't hate them."

—Sam Harris

THE greater good

OJ Simpson, Bernie Madoff, Donald Sterling, Elliot Rodger (all fated to be in the villain role) did not have a free will (I hope that this is crystal clear now) and you agree with me because you now understand causal will or causal chains of will (karmic streams etc.).

    2 Everything has a cause and every cause has a cause so on and so forth (conscious, un/subconscious doesn't matter). As long as you agree that there were in fact causes that caused these people above to be in these horrific scandals can we finally now say we are on the same page (the no free will page that is). Whether or not these people or their advisors (or parents, or spouses, or therapists or social workers) even knew what caused them to

behave the way they did is immaterial to these teachings. The point is everything has to have a cause and we did not originate or start the causal chain of our lives (our parents had sex).

3   Therefore, if either you or I were born into his (any villains name here) body at the exact moment of his conception under the same exact circumstances (and grew up the same exact way he did), you too would have gotten yourself fated and stuck in the same exact mess he found himself in (causal chain).
4   In other words, the same exact life he had, looking exactly like him, same personality, and same exact overall life circumstances. Same mind and soul.
5   Same nature, same nurture, same genetics, same socialization, same opportunity to cheat (Madoff), same conditioning, same morals, etc.
6   Same biology (atom for atom, neuron for neuron), same environment etc. etc. -- you get the idea by now. The reasons why he did his so called "evil" crimes could have happened and would have happened to you or me just as easily.
7   We too would have been labeled an "evil monster" and been cast by God/the universe in the "villain roll" in this predetermined movie called life on planet earth.
8   Always remember that free will is a myth and an illusion when you are judging another human being's behaviors and actions.
9   Always remember that people often become stuck and check mate themselves to points or a point in their lives that is always "I had no other choice, there was nothing else I could do at the time (with the knowledge I had at the time) to do what I did." Elliot Rodger himself said "humanity forced my hand" in his manifesto. Rest assured, if Elliot Rodger could have done otherwise, he would have.
10 This is also true for Steve Bartman. Steve Bartman was the fan who interfered with a catchable ball in the 2003 Chicago Cubs playoff game against the Florida Marlins.
11 What about Bill Buckner of the 1986 Game 6 Mets vs Red Sox botched grounder behind the first base bag? All people mentioned in this new kind of Bible (Madoff, Bartman, Buckner, Elliot Rodger, Don Sterling etc.) acted without free will. Same could be said about people like Monica Lewinsky,

Chris McCandless, OJ Simpson, Tanya Harding, Hitler, or Jeffrey Dahmer. Same could be said about everybody on planet earth. Good or evil doesn't matter. Mother Teresa's will was obviously also not free.

12 Rest assured, what happened to the people mentioned above did not happen to them because of their free will. If you were them, it would have happened to you the same exact way.
13 The Greater Good

This new kind of Holy Bible's teachings (when properly understood) are for the greater good and for the betterment of the general welfare for society at large. Bernie Madoff's son Mark committed suicide because (we assume) of the shame he felt.

14 If he knew his father didn't have a free will, I don't think he would have felt so incredibly bad about the whole situation.
15 He would still feel badly yes (very badly I'm sure), just not as terrible as he apparently felt (driven to kill himself).
16 This new kind of Holy Bible aims to expose the belief in free will as pure myth and illusion—a spot light on all of humanity so that the essential understanding of this myth/illusion will hopefully make emotions less severe and intense. This will be achieved by human beings understanding that people fundamentally are neither "blameworthy nor praiseworthy."
17 Compassion for your fellow man will rule society and not blame. Though we must "act as if" we have free will as a conventionally pragmatic and useful tool that will keep and maintain a civil society, people will understand that an undercurrent of "sympathy for the fated role" one is destined to play out will make truly and deeply blaming and stigmatizing others and most importantly truly and fundamentally blaming oneself almost impossible to do.
18 Your only job in this futuristic society will be to try and to find out why the universe cast this roll upon you. You cannot even blame the universe or fate for whatever happens to you because it too does not possess a free will.

"It is what it is."

—The Reality Teller

19 Fundamentally, the only thing they did wrong was be a human being (and obviously not have a free will).

"The fundamental premise of REBT therapy is that behaviors are caused by what people believe about the situations they face. REBT proposes a 'bio-psycho-social' explanation of how humans come to feel and behave; that is to say, that Ellis also believed biological, and social factors along with cognitive factors are involved in the experiencing and acting process. This point is important because it suggests there are limits as to how much a person can change. This is why REBT therapy fails so much of the time. By Ellis suggesting that there are limits to as to how much a person can change is an admission that free will doesn't exist. The reason is simple. If we all had a free will, we would all be easily cured by such a thing as REBT therapy. We would simply 'choose' our beliefs to be different."

—The Reality Teller

"Most, if not all talk therapy is inherently flawed. This is because most therapists assume you have something called free will. You can't blame them for being this way. This is what they were taught."

—The Reality Teller

"The reality is this: Rebt therapy, cognitive behavior therapy, and almost all talk therapy (all based on free will) are all obsessed with people being 'rational.' There is nothing more irrational than believing in free will."

—The Reality Teller

"Much like climate change, free will being an illusion is apparently another inconvenient truth. I think a movie clearly explaining the illusion of free will needs to be made."

—The Reality Teller

"This is the way it has to be."

—The Reality Teller

"All the prior events have led up to this moment."

—The Reality Teller

"This moment is exactly as it should be given what has happened before."

—The Reality Teller

The Holy Bible: No Free Will. Amen.

Book Thirteen by The Reflector

The Book of

Reflections

Chapter One

REFLECT on this for a few moments: We have been incorrectly conditioned as a society to believe in free will and it is simply time for some truth.

"If the word freedom means truth then we have more freedom in believing that determinism (zero free will) is the truth."

—The Reflector

"Most of us grew up believing we have a free will. We had no choice but to grow up all wrong."

—The Reflector

"The truth that everything is fated and predetermined will set you free."

—The Reflector

"Upon proper reflection of your life, you will soon agree that everything that happened to you had to have happened to you at the exact time, place, and moment that it did. There was no escape from it."

—The Reflector

2. Transcending the illusion of free will would represent a huge leap in the evolution of our consciousness and would forever alter the landscape of how humans think about being human.
3. The atmosphere of our planet evolved over hundreds of millions of years as a product of the activities of simple early life forms and it simply kept evolving to the state we find it in today. Some call it global warming, some call it climate change, while others are saying this is the beginning of the "green energy" revolution.
4. Either way, the atmosphere and harnessing its energy for human use was always evolving and is always evolving and will always be evolving. Why should human consciousness be the only thing not evolving? The answer is that of course it is evolving, for it is also not a static thing.
5. Evolution of consciousness is happening every day as more and more people are beginning to realize what a farce this whole "I have free will" thing is.
6. Upon proper reflection, you will soon agree that believing in this magical thing called "free will" is simply nuts.
7. People love to take the free will thing both ways. Free will flip flopping or double talk seems to be the way most people get though life. They have or have not free will when it is most convenient for them to do so.

"Free will is tempting to believe in. It is tempting to believe that our minds float 'free' -- independent and high above our conditioning, training, and practicing. But this belief is completely at odds with everything science has learned in molecular biology and neuroscience."

—The Reflector

"Neuroscience is changing the way we think about ourselves. If physical processes in the brain cause all of our beliefs, thoughts, and actions, then how can there be free will?"

—The Reflector

"I challenge you to reflect on your life. Reflect on your so-called 'free' choices. You will soon realize after proper reflection that everything had to happen exactly the way it did. I'm The Reflector and please reflect on that. Thank you."

—The Reflector

The Holy Bible: No Free Will. Amen.

Chapter Two

REALITY isn't the way you wish things to be, nor the way they appear to be (that is what an illusion is), but the way things actually are. Either you acknowledge reality and use it to your benefit or simply live in the deluded state that free will exists (the way most of us are currently living). The best thing about not believing in free will is that severe and intense blame and resentment go away almost instantly.

2. Upon proper reflection we can understand how exactly our decisions are made.
3. Our decision to take one action as opposed to another relies on the complex choreographed dance between many different processes in the prefrontal cortex and an entire spectrum of internal states of the body such as changes in our heart rate, breathing rate, temperature, muscle tone, *somato-sensory system, and especially our feelings and emotions.
4. As we go through life we pay attention to how interacting with people and things makes us feel.
5. It is entirely based on our causal past.
6. Some things feel good to us on the inside while others do not. We are always taking notes.

"We attach pain or pleasure to everything we do and definitely prefer pleasure. Rocket science this isn't. Upon proper reflection, people incorrectly believe in free will because it is more pleasurable for them to do so. Reflect on that for a few moments before you continue reading this fine new kind of Bible."

—The Reflector

*The somato-sensory system is a diverse sensory system composed of the receptors and processing centers to produce the sensory modalities such as touch, temperature, proprioception (body position), and nociception (pain). The sensory receptors cover the skin and epithelia, skeletal muscles, bones and joints, internal organs, and the cardiovascular system.

The Holy Bible: No Free Will. Amen.

Book Fourteen by The Reporter

The Book of
Man Does Not Have Free Will

Chapter One

Evolution can be scary. Evolution might not be understood and may be poorly judged. But, to evolve is to change to better oneself and to always be open to new ideas. The major thrust of this work, The Holy Bible: No Free Will is to establish at long last that free will is pure illusion.

    2   Different times call for different minds

Just like we once all thought the world was flat or that the earth was the center of the solar system, we must now all come to a point collectively and realize that free will is a grand hoax, a grand illusion, and a grand myth. Quite simply stated, mankind has been duped.

    3   One of the most important lessons of them all is to understand the difference between the **fundamental reality** of your life and the **pragmatic reality** of your life.
    4   There is a huge difference between the fundamental and the pragmatic, and understanding this difference is job number one

if you are to fully understand and internalize the teachings of this book -- The Holy Bible: No Free Will.

5 The question of whether or not we have "free will" has been hiding in academic circles and philosophy classes for thousands and thousands of years. It is now time to take this matter straight to the heart and center of Main Street on Truth Avenue.

6 The people now need to know the truth. The truth is this: **Man Does Not Have Free Will.**

"Life is predetermined and is just a matter of fate. Nothing is up to us and we are just along for the ride."

—The Reporter

The Holy Bible: No Free Will. Amen.

Chapter Two

YOU either have free will or you don't. Many people love to tell me "I have a little free will." I need to report to you the following: There is no in between or grey area.

2. You either have it or you don't. There is no "I have a little free will." It's a black or white issue. The best we can do for the time being (the transition period from free will to no free will) is to know we have zero (otherwise known as 0%) free will, but act as if we have free will. This is the most honest approach available to us at this time.
3. Eventually and gradually in time as society begins to get used to these teachings, and as an entire new vocabulary gradually gets created (such as blameless or faultless responsibility), will society be ready to graduate to the next level.
4. The people of tomorrow will understand and be compelled by the entire universe to know why it's impossible for us to have free will (after reading this new kind of Bible for example), and will no longer expect other people or themselves for that matter to walk around simply pretending to have one.
5. At that time, "acting as if" we have free will, will come across as just being plain silly.
6. So here is a quick snapshot or example of how society will improve once all the teachings of The Holy Bible: No Free Will are understood.

Human Emotions with Free Will 100% Positive we have 'Free' Will and believe so does everyone else Model	Human Emotions without Free Will Know we have zero 'Free' Will
Self-Blame	Blame Fate not ourselves
Other Blame	Blame fate not other person(s)
Self-Hatred	Fundamental Self- Innocence
Other Hatred	Fundamental Other - Innocence
Severe and Intense Anxiety	Mild Concern
Severe and Intense Depression	Mild Sadness
Severe and Intense Shame	Mild Disappointment

Severe and Intense Guilt	Mild Remorse
Severe and Intense Resentment	Mild Resentment
Severe and Intense Hurt	Mild Sorrow
Severe and Intense Anger	Mild Anger
Severe and Intense Jealousy	Mild Jealousy
Arrogance	Humility
Look what I did! I deserve a medal!	By the Grace of God or compelled by the entirety of the universe = with gratitude
What a terrible thing I did, I deserve to die!	My actions were compelled by Fate = I am fundamentally innocent.
I'm a Hero	Timing intersected with good preparation - By the Grace of God or compelled by the entirety of the universe
I'm a Villain	Timing intersected with poor preparation. It is what it is. I was fated for this to happen and I'm curious to know why. I am fundamentally innocent.

7   As you can see from above:

One reality—the "free will" reality shows human emotions as "severe and intense." The other reality -- the one without free will shows human emotions as more mild and muted:

8   The world without "free will" has a much better chance of being a kinder, more gentle, placid, calmer and serene place.
9   Religion, conventional morality, and the criminal justice system, at least as practiced today, owe much of their underpinning to an unexamined faith in a traditionally conceived free will model of society. That is about to change.
10 You may notice that some of the teachers go back and forth between the so called "pragmatic" and the so called "fundamental."
11 Some Definitions

Pragmatic means how human beings may aspire to act or behave, but not as they actually believe to be true deep in their hearts. What is the most economical way to be in terms of time, effort, and energy? What is easiest thing to do versus what is the truth of the matter? What is the pragmatic nature of a human being?

Pragmatic Synonyms:

Sensible, businesslike, commonsensical, down-to-earth, efficient, hardheaded, logical, matter-of-fact, practical, reasonable, commonsense, hardheaded, matter-of-fact, mundane, no-nonsense, plainspoken

> 12 Fundamental means what human beings actually believe to be true deep in their hearts and what their core essence is. What is their true nature and what they cannot help but do? What is the fundamental nature of a human being?

Fundamental - Synonyms

Basically, centrally, essentially, inevitably, certainly, accordingly, as a matter of course, automatically, axiomatically, beyond one's control, by definition, by its own nature, cardinally, compulsorily, essentially, alone as such, by and of itself, by definition, by its very nature, by itself fundamentally, in essence in itself

"I don't believe in free will. Not because I'm probabilistic, a compatibilist, an incompatibilist, a determinist, an indeterminist, a predeterminist, or any other fancy word you can think of. I don't believe in free will because I'm a realist."

—The Reporter

"You have nothing to lose by reading The Holy Bible: No Free Will because the only thing you'll be losing is your sense of having a free will which you never had in the first place."

—The Reporter

"Let's get the free will debate out of academia and philosophy class and straight to Main Street. In case you get lost on your way there, that's next to Front and Center Street on Truth Ave."

—The Reporter

"We have been bamboozled to incorrectly believe that we have a free will."

—The Reporter

"Every moment of the universe is dependent on the moment before. Human lives are no different."

—The Reporter

"Human beings are part of (in) the universe not outside it. Have you ever gone to the beach on a starry night and looked up and said to yourself 'gee I'm outside of the universe?'

I highly doubt it. Therefore, it is safe to say we are in the universe and must adhere to all the laws of the universe. The first law of the universe is this: Every moment of the universe is dependent on the moment before. Therefore every moment of a human life is dependent on the moment before. This is the causal chain of reality in a nutshell."

—Nick Vale

- God gave man 'free will' is the ultimate in nonsense.
- God gave man the ability to write a more accurate Holy Bible (the one you are currently reading) than the Holy Bible He supposedly wrote.
- God didn't write any books Himself. The authors of scripture were fallible human beings. They wrote books supposedly as conduits of God's will. The same can be said of all that is written here. Nick Vale is just as much a conduit of God's will as the authors of the Old and New Testament. Same can be said for every human being.

- People love to say . . . "God knows everything and yet I have free will." Well which is it? It's like saying my flight is delayed and on time.
- People love to say "I have a little free will—say 1% of me."
- So that 1% of you that is 100% independent of your genetics and past experiences (nature and nurture) would make a decision based on what exactly?

"If I truly had a free will, I could wake up tomorrow and decide to become a Russian ice hockey player even though I can't play ice hockey and I'm not Russian . . . You see to have a 'free' will means there would be no causality to anything . . . actually I'd rather be a Canadian player—I think they're a little better these days. No wait . . . I'd rather be a French nuclear submarine captain . . . no wait I'd rather be a real life James Bond . . . no wait . . . and Italian Chef . . . no wait . . . a French Chef . . . no wait . . . I'd like to be a Portuguese soccer star . . . no actually a Spanish soccer star, no wait a Greek fisherman, . . . you see . . . with a free will I could just keep changing my mind over and over again because without causality . . . I could be anything I chose to be. All choices are now exactly 50/50—it's no wonder I can't make up my mind on what to do next."

—Nick Vale

The Holy Bible: No Free Will. Amen.

Book Fifteen by The Reviewer

The Book of
Review

Chapter One

ONE thing leads to another -- how about some truth? Wouldn't you agree that given a choice people would prefer to hear the truth than be lied to?

You are never fundamentally blameworthy. You are never fundamentally praiseworthy. You can be pragmatically blameworthy and you can be pragmatically praiseworthy however.

- Time for a paradigm shift. Time for the evolution of consciousness.
- I'm sick and tired of people taking life both ways. Free will flip flopping is out of control. There is seemingly no end to this hypocritical double talk. Look what I did! I deserve a medal, a raise etc. Deaths or bad things happen and we hear God did this to me, why is God doing this to me? Good things I do with my free will, but bad things I blame on other people or God does (no free will)?

- All action and thought is dependent on the moment before it.
- Neither praiseworthy nor blameworthy. Free will is a myth of epic proportions and a huge monster secretly ruling our society.
- Cause and effect, cause and effect, cause and effect, cause and effect, cause and effect, cause and effect. Cause and effect, cause and effect, cause and effect, cause and effect, cause and effect, cause and effect. Cause and effect, cause and effect, cause and effect, cause and effect, cause and effect, cause and effect.
- Training, Conditioning or Practicing = creating grooves in your brain's neuro-pathways. Preferences are built up over time. Preferences go from partial preferences (back and forth, then picking vanilla slightly more often than chocolate) to full preferences (always picking vanilla). Preferences are built up over time as likes and dislikes become more apparent to oneself.
- Genetics and Environment (nature and nurture) are always conditioning you, away from pain towards pleasure (you have no choice but to always seek out overall greater satisfaction). See book number twenty three called Quick Summary.
- Act "as if" you have a free will for the time being for pragmatic reasons.
- Mark Madoff must have felt terrible and intense shame, but if he understood that his father didn't have free will, maybe he wouldn't have felt so bad and would still be alive today.
- Be mad at the Universe/Cosmos/God not at another person for their wills are not free.
- Bio Social model -- nature and nurture condition you.
- Play your role.
- True Nature of Reality.
- Classical Conditioning/Training, Operant Conditioning/Training, and many various other conditioning models all exist in reality. Everything falls into one conditioning model or another.
- The Causal Will.
- All humans get programmed like super complicated robots.

- The smallest difference in mindset -- even a .00000000000000000000001% change can create a "butterfly effect." This is a tiny change on the smallest of levels that can cause a massive "ripple out" effect. So from a "butterfly" to a "ripple out" can in fact create a huge difference is the mindset of an entire society.
- Ripple Out Effect = More compassion and more understanding. Blame Universe/Cosmos/God not the other person. If you blame his or her parents, they will in turn blame their parents so on and so forth with no end in sight.
- Adam blamed Eve and Eve blamed the snake.
- Music is a great example to jar memories -- some songs make you think of certain times in your life and create certain emotions within you. Why is that? The answer is called "conditioning."
- Invisible causes or pressures: Pleasure versus Pain. Hedonic Imperative, Fairness Imperative, Moral Imperative, Optimization Imperative etc. To be liked. To be a hero. Financial pressure, relationship pressure, and pressure to do the right thing. Pressure is an invisible cause.
- What caused you to read this book? What caused that? And what caused that before that?
- All criminals and "mentally ill" are fundamentally innocent. More compassion and understanding is needed.
  During the planet's transitional phase from free will to no free will it may be best to act "as if" you have a free will for pragmatic reasons. Eventually when everyone understands that man's will is not free, we will no longer have to "act as if" we have free will as that will seem silly once everyone is finally on board.
- Conditioning and Causality determine what you believe because it was what you were taught or not taught.
- Neuroscientists increasingly believe that our will is not free.
- Each moment dependent on prior moment culminating in a particular action, behavior or decision.
- All real action is happening at the level of the synapses and neurotransmitters.
- You are nothing but a pack of neurons.

- How can you over-ride your genetic and environmental factors? The answer is you cannot.
- Free will contradicts cause and effect science.
- Our sense of free will is deeply ingrained.
- Belief in free will is the default setting currently in our western culture.
- All mental states including belief and desire have neurobiological underpinnings.
- People are simply intoxicated with the idea that they have free will, totally inebriated and illogical.
- If free will existed, why wouldn't everyone just choose to do good?
- Babies don't have free will so when exactly do we start to have it? If so -- how would you know?
- Different minds for different times.
- Every moment dependent on prior moment.
- Free Will is a Mythical Monster of Epic proportions.
- You are neither fundamentally blameworthy nor fundamentally praiseworthy. Understand the difference between the pragmatic and the fundamental.
- It's all about training and conditioning, Classical and Operant etc.
- Main Street now needs to know the truth about their wills. Philosophy class and esoteric academic circles need to now come to the people with the truth about the illusion of free will. It is time for the people to finally know the truth about their human causal wills based on their personal history.
- As stated above, this debate needs to go mainstream and out of the philosophy classrooms and academia. It's been debated behind closed doors for over 2000 years.
- Major thrust is this: We aim to establish at long last a determinist position that addresses and effectively refutes traditional as well as popular contemporary arguments supporting the freedom of human willing
- Religion, education, conventional morality, and criminal justice alike, at least as practiced today in the USA owes much of its underpinnings to an unexamined faith in traditionally conceived free will. We hear it all the time on the news, in our

songs and movies, on TV shows and selling newspapers. People love to hear about so called "heroes" and so called "villains."

- It's not that good and evil don't exist, they do. It's just that certain people are just playing the roles of good and evil and they couldn't help themselves. It was all fated and G-d is/was and will be the fundamental and ultimate casting director in this theater we call planet earth.
- The invisible hand of fate is always at play. Otherwise known as karma.
- Our actions should be based on the ever—present awareness that humans in their thinking, feeling and acting are not free, but are as causally bound. Deeds are done, and events happen but free will is just an illusion.
- The mind is predetermined to wish for this or that by a cause, which has also been predetermined by another cause, and this again by another, and so on to infinity. This insight teaches us to hate no one, to despise no one, to make fun of no one, to be angry with no one, and to envy no one.
- Any crime, no matter how heinous it was, can be traced back to the antecedent conditions acting through the accused's physiology, heredity, and environment. Crime = C. So there's C - 1, C - 2, C - 3, C - 4, C - 5, C - 6 regressed all the way back to the beginning of time. The numbers just equal moments.
- Randomness — Our actions are determined, in which case we are not responsible for them, or they are the result of random events, in which case we are also not responsible for them. Either way, we are not responsible for them and there will be no judgment day forthcoming.
- Our ignorance of "causal chains" leads us to believe we have free will. Many causes hide in the sub/unconscious.
- Free will flip flopping is what most people do. They say they have free will whenever it serves them the best, and say they don't have a free will for the same exact reason. How convenient. Free will being an illusion is a very "inconvenient truth" for many people.
- Our arguments refuting "free" will, will remain undefeated for the rest of time.

- If human beings evolved from animals as many people believe and animals don't have free will, then how on earth did humans get this magical thing?
- The truth is nothing can happen without a cause or a reason. Causal regression takes us back before we were born. We did not self - cause ourselves. Our parents caused us with something called sexual intercourse. Furthermore, there is always a cause to the cause stretching back to before the earth was born, and regressing all the way back to the beginning of time.
- You don't have to fundamentally blame a flat tire to fix it. Likewise, you don't have to deeply or truly or fundamentally blame a human being (and send to hell for all of eternity) to keep society safe. Pragmatic "blame" is all you need.

The Holy Bible: No Free Will. Amen.

Book Sixteen by The Simplifier

The Book of

150 Quotes

Chapter One

ALL quotes are by The Simplifier

"This year is a lot like 1492. The ridiculous notions that the world was flat and free will existed were both shattered."

    2 "We are constantly *feeling as if* we are making uncaused decisions. This makes life *feel like* we have a free will. In reality, we are constantly advancing and evolving our consciousness like explorers into deep space. We have finally discovered and landed on another planet with life. This planet is called The New Earth and everyone on it now knows the truth about free will being an illusion."

    3 *"Every second of your life is business. The business of trying to attain a perceived fair exchange of human energy. We seek value for value in everything we do. We have no choice in the matter."

    4 "Believing in free will is a lot like smoking. It's addictive, bad for you, and a really hard habit to break. If you smoke and can't

---

* Please see my book "Enlightenment Through Entitlement" to learn much more about why we (human beings) have no choice (no free will) but to seek a perceived fair exchange of our precious human energy in all our affairs.

stop, no worries. Being a smoker was predetermined (it wasn't up to you). But, if you're going to smoke, you might as well be a causal chain smoker."

5 "Refuting free will with 'causal chain will theory' is as loophole free and as airtight as it gets."

6 "At first thought, The New Earth without free will feels foreign, strange, and dangerous. Gradually, slowly, and in time we have no choice but to become the best of friends."

7 "We are all in this together. The very least we can do is get this free will issue correct once and for all. The planet will soon unite and finally agree that everything has a cause. It's quite important actually since it only pertains to the reality of everything. Getting the fundamental reality of life correct is the least we can do while we are here don't you think?"

8 *"Your unfree selfish will has no choice but to understand that every moment of your life is business. The business of getting a perceived fair exchange of human energy. The problem is people most often disagree on what the word 'fair' means. This is where issues of entitlement and deservedness are hiding and when the inevitable fighting begins."

9 "This book is indeed revolutionary. These are the times for humanity to overcome, and greatly benefit from overcoming the illusion of free will. We shall overcome, we shall overcome, we shall overcome someday. Sounds a little familiar doesn't it?"

10 "If I truly had a free will, I would choose to be a perfect angel always. How come I can't just choose the exact right words at this moment to explain that even better?"

11 "If you get in an argument with someone who believes in free will ask them to give an example of what they believe to have been a freely chosen choice. Let them answer. Then ask them what the cause of that was. Congratulations you have just won the argument. I'm the simplifier and it's that simple."

12 "Randomness is clearly not free will. Please do not insult your intelligence and argue this point in public. If you believe everything is random as a defense to why there is free will, it's best to keep it to yourself."

13 "We're born into a world of cause and effect. Once again, I'm The Simplifier and it's really that simple."

---

* Please see my book "Enlightenment Through Entitlement" to learn much more about why we (human beings) have no choice (no free will) but to seek a perceived fair exchange of our precious human energy in all our affairs.

14 "Morality, fairness, pleasure, pain, sex drive, ego, genetics, biology, physics, quantum physics, randomness, chaos theory, the uncertainty principle, the subconscious, the unconscious, *the feeling of* making decisions, I want this and that, I desire this and that, I make decisions, I do what I want to do and I don't do what I don't want to do, we could go on for hours. Let's save some trees and just say none of this will ever prove free will exists."

15 "If free will exists prove it already. The onus of proof is not only on the non—free will believers. The truth is the only way to absolutely prove free will would be to have a time machine and go back in time. Rewind the entire universe and press play. To prove free will, everything would have to happen differently than it actually did (everything including people could have and would have done otherwise)."

16 "What caused you to read this line number sixteen? Everything has to have a cause."

17 "Life is actually much better without a free will once you get the hang of it. When others or we are compelled by the universe or fate to do wrong, we can no longer fundamentally blame them or ourselves. Furthermore, when others or ourselves do something really great we won't feel envious or become too arrogant."

18 "Without free will, the pain of resentment and guilt should melt away like an ice cube on a beautiful warm sunny day."

19 "In the new causal will society, less intense emotions will still exist due to the *human energy balancing machinery that we were all born to be, and we have no choice but to accept this truth of our existence."

20 "If you do something wrong, please no longer compound your anguish and blame yourself. Your will was not free. You had no choice but to do what you did."

21 "Life is like watching a movie for the very first time that you're both the star of and the observer of."

22 "The discoveries of This Newer Testament (The Holy Bible: No Free Will) will make all other discoveries look inconsequential by comparison. See www.nofreewill.info or www.nofreewill.org

---

*learn this concept in my book "Enlightenment Through Entitlement"

23 "If free will existed, why anyone would choose a life of crime? Why would anyone choose to suffer? Why would anyone commit suicide due to personal suffering? Why not just choose to be happy all the time?"
24 "The acting 'as if' we have a free will even though we don't have one is the most important dialectic in the history of the world that needs to be synthesized. This can only be accomplished by understanding the *universe compelled pragmatic pursuits of perceived fair exchange(s) of human energy justice system"
25 "I like my odds on siding with the truth. 10 times out of 10, the truth just feels better."
26 A person who believes in free will is basically saying the following:

"I don't want realism. I want fantasy and magic. I don't tell the truth. I tell what I wish were true or what ought to be the truth. I believe in magic. Magic and fantasy are my best friends."

27 "All criminals are pragmatically guilty and fundamentally innocent."
28 "Nothing, including this book, is 100% original. Everything influences everything else. People simply expand on things where others left off."
29 "The formulation of ideologies is observable throughout the world's history. The Hitler movement was clearly a misguided ideology. Same is true for human being's having a free will."
30 "There are many invisible pressures in life which cause decision making. Economic pressures, financial pressures, relationship pressures, wanting to fit in pressures, wanting to be liked pressures, climate pressures (what to wear), time pressures etc. etc. Wills are never uncaused."
31 Person A says "I am angry. I am jealous."

Person B says "What are the causes of your anger and jealousy."

---

* learn this concept in my book "Enlightenment Through Entitlement"

32 "Propaganda, brainwashing, advertising, suggestions, recommendations from friends and family are all forms of cause and effect conditioning."
33 "Memories of experiences are effects which influence future causal will chain decision making."
34 "Learning about a non-free will based society is a lot like buying a good stock or investment. As time goes on, it will appreciate in value."
35 "Investing in a free will society at this point in time is like investing in the horse and buggy just as the car was invented. Or investing in candles just as the light bulb was invented."
36 "How could the mind and body be completely and instantly free from its past in order to make so called free will decisions?"
37 "Saying your will is free is like saying all your prior accumulation of psychological and emotional knowledge, and experience is suddenly and completely irrelevant."
38 "To see things as they actually are is much nobler than lying to oneself."
39 "Society has conditioned us to falsely believe that our wills are free."
40 "Without the right foundation, society will never evolve to the truth about reality. A free will based society simply has the wrong foundation."
41 "The free will issue needs to be looked at objectively. People have trouble doing this because it feels better to most people to believe in free will. Therefore, it is safe to say, the jury in this matter (the people) are biased from the moment the topic is mentioned (they are biased in favor of free will existing because they desperately want it to be true). This is why the universe keeps losing in this matter. Let's just stick to the facts please people and leave all emotion out of it. The Universe vs The People rests its case your honor. The Universe claims that the people have it all wrong about the nature of man's will and the universe will be proven correct."
42 "The facts are simple. Cause and effect. We rest our case."
43 "You have a will, it just isn't free."
44 "Past pain or pleasure has a continuity to it. It sustains and nourishes all present and future decision making."

45 "What's the cause or causes of why you are sitting in the particular chair you are currently sitting in as you read this?"

46 "If you're not sitting at this moment, what's the cause or causes as to why you are standing?"

47 "In the long run, people will find it takes less human energy to simply admit the truth about their unfree causally chained wills. Are the people of the future really going to expend all their effort in keeping the truth about reality a secret for the rest of time? Keeping the truth out will soon take double and triple barricading your doors (minds). I think it'll be much more peaceful to instead just open the door and warmly invite the truth in."

48 "The truth about the unfree will should not be looked at as an enemy coming to steal your house away. Instead, the truth about the unfree will should be invited in like a long lost love or family member in desperate need of a good hot meal and a warm bed. It would be most wise to let this person in with open arms. You might as well be polite and courteous to your new house guest because I have a feeling they're going to stay a while (how does for the rest of time sound?)"

49 "Admitting the truth about our unfree wills is a lot less depressing than secretly knowing we are all living a life of lies."

50 "A free will based society is like a Ponzi scheme or a house of cards. A total collapse is inevitable. It's not a question of if it will collapse; it's only a question of when."

51 "Unfortunately for those people protecting the old way of life (those who believe in free will), they don't make people like they used to. People in this day and age are now armed with something called the Internet from birth. The people of tomorrow won't be dumb enough or stupid enough to believe in free will. Consciousness is always evolving and the soon to be tipping point of truth is well on its way."

52 "Are you really dumb enough to believe that your decisions are independent of your previous causes and effects and your conditioning?"

53 "Random behavior is not free will. Nice try though."

54 "There's a lot of confusion of what the word free means. It's a free country and I have free speech. I am here to tell you that our

wills aren't free. Feel free to try and refute me. I look forward to our free flowing debate. Invite your family and friends and tell them the debate will be free of charge."

55 "Sinners are merely poorly programmed human computers. They are not to blame because they weren't in charge of the programming."

56 "No one has ever described a manner in which mental and physical events could arise uncaused."

57 "What a relief to discover that I no longer have to fundamentally blame myself for all the silly and stupid mistakes that I've made. Thank God for this new kind of Bible of the no free will variety."

58 "Since the great majority of people on earth believe they have a free will, this book will most likely be received with some backlash. The more you are in protest of what is written here, the more likely this book is correct. Change is almost always scary, unsettling, and threatening and there is no choice in the matter.

59 "Not having free will is a game changer. It's a whole new ballgame now."

60 "A causal will society is the foundation of a saner and more truthful world."

61 "If you can't see the truth of the causal chains in your life, perhaps it's time you had your mind and eyes examined."

62 *"Believing in free will most likely escalates violence and wars instead of simply talking it out. The people of the future will have no choice but to sit down and negotiate perceived fair exchanges of human energy instead of being so quick to bomb each other."

63 "How can it be that I can walk on the Upper West Side of Manhattan, New York and know that 80% of the people that I am looking at are Democrats without ever needing to actually get to know them? Likewise if I were in Idaho, I could say just the opposite and assume that 80% are Republicans. Is this phenomena some sort of inexplicable accident or is there some sort of causal chain conformity conditioning going on here?

64 "There are no such things as pure accidents since everything has a cause or multiple causes. All one needs to do is regress the

---

* Please see my book "Enlightenment Through Entitlement" to learn much more about why we (human beings) have no choice (no free will) but to seek a perceived fair exchange of our precious human energy in all our affairs.

chain of causes all the way back to the creation of the universe and blame The First Causer (if there even was one).
I can assure you this—The First Causer was not a human being because human beings were not here first. The universe is about 14 billion years old. A human being did not, cannot, and will not first cause anything."

65 "It's much more reasonable and rational to not believe in free will."
66 *"'From this day forward, there shall be no more cringing at the words selfish, selfishness, or anything that pertains to a human being wanting what's in his or her best self-interest. Put in its proper perspective, being selfish 100% of the time is reality. It is 100% selfish to only desire perceived fair exchanges of human energy otherwise known as value for value interactions every second of every human life."
67 "There is nothing more noble and truthful than admitting and openly acknowledging that human beings always act in their own self-interest."
68 "The word sacrifice does not mean what most people think it means. There is no such thing as a sacrifice or sacrificing. What is actually involved in 'sacrificing' is that a person is acting on the belief that the good one hopes to receive in return (for the so called sacrifice) will be worth what one expends in doing something for the other person or cause. Some examples of the expenditure are time, effort, human energy, money, risking one's life etc. In the case of risking one's life to save another, many people instinctively feel it's better to try and rescue the other person than have to live with the guilt that another died or was severely injured whom you might have otherwise been able to save."
69 "The exact same sentence above could be used for the words altruism, martyrs and charity work."
70 "A proper and honest assessment of reality is the building block that will allow the evolution of consciousness to blossom in a society desperate for truth."
71 "A realist is a person who believes in basing his life on facts as opposed to basing his entire life on anything that seems illusory, mythical, fantasy driven, or magical."

---

* Please see my book "Enlightenment Through Entitlement" to learn much more about why we (human beings) have no choice (no free will) but to seek a perceived fair exchange of our precious human energy in all our affairs.

72 "Reality isn't the way you wish things to be, nor the way they appear to be, but the way they actually are."

73 "Each person does perceive reality differently, but reality could care less. There is a truth to reality. 2 + 2 = 4. People might perceive that 2 + 2 = 5, but it is their perception of the reality that is incorrect. Reality doesn't fit to your perception.
It's the other way around as you try to match your perception to reality."

74 "The people in your life who most dread the widespread knowledge of the reality that people always act in their own self—interest are most likely the people in your life who you are currently acting in their best self—interest. They're the ones with the most to lose once you have this information and they will try to keep you down as long as humanly possible. The same is true for free will believers. Free will believers will try as hard as they can to keep the truth (no free will) from disturbing their illusory worlds from collapsing around them. Beware: they are VERY attached to their free will belief system. They actually truly believe they are fundamentally responsible for all the good and success in their lives. Some of them may even fight this idea that free will doesn't exist to the death."

75 "If we had a free will, why would anyone choose suffering? If we had a free will, why would someone be redundant (like me)?"

76 "Everything that happens is predetermined and fated to be so. The exact moment of your death is predetermined."

77 "We're really spectators of our own lives, watching them unfold."

78 "Our civilization will not crumble by our transcending the illusion of free will."

79 "Relationships with other people improve by perceiving our wills as causal rather than free."

80 "Understanding the true nature of the human will minimizes blame, guilt, arrogance and envy."

81 "State of the universe causality is most basic refutation of free will."

82 *"Understanding our wills as causal does not give us license to do as we want. We must understand the concept of a universe compelled pragmatic system of pursuits of perceived

---

* Please see my book "Enlightenment Through Entitlement" to learn much more about why we (human beings) have no choice (no free will) but to seek a perceived fair exchange of our precious human energy in all our affairs.

fair exchanges of human energy justice system. Each society for each time period of human history has been compelled by the universe to declare certain behaviors and in some cases certain thoughts as unlawful and unjust."

83 "Our strongest motivation will result in the action we choose at that particular moment in time."

84 "Even if we define our thoughts as 'spiritual' they are still subject to cause and effect conditioning. Nothing is immune to this law."

85 "Quantum mechanics is completely causal. Probabilities arise from underlying causality."

86 "Preferences determine our decisions; we do not choose what our preferences are."

87 "We are predetermined to choose what seems most reasonable to us at the time."

88 "Change is the most basic process in the universe. It is completely causal."

89 "Some of us believe we have a partially free will. Which choices would be free and which would not? How would you even know the difference?"

90 "All people in jail or prison are fundamentally innocent."

91 "Try to think of one thought for a few minutes at a time - it is impossible and reveals that your will is not free."

92 "Our entire civilization is based on the false premise that we human beings have a free will."

93 "We are hard-wired to seek pleasure and avoid pain."

94 "I don't understand myself at all, for I really want to do what is right, but I can't. Sometimes I do things that I don't want to do and I have no idea why I do them . . . What in the world is going on here? Our feelings and moods determine our decisions; we do not freely choose our feelings and moods."

95 "There is usually more than one reason or cause for a choice."

96 "Moral decisions are mostly based on what is taught to us throughout our lives. We do not choose what was taught to us growing up. Parents in different cultures and in different time periods simply teach their children different things."

97 "Transcending the illusion of free will would represent a huge leap in the evolution of our consciousness."

98 "Even If quantum behavior is random, that fact would not support the position of free will."

99 "The belief in free will is like our hand believing it is responsible for what it does."

100 "Our strongest desire will determine our decision."

101 "Reasons and causes always occur before their effects. The effects linger around and influence future reasons and causes."

102 "Whatever happens to us each day has been meant to have happened to us from the beginning of time."

103 "We simply cannot choose to do otherwise. If we could have, we would have. Plain and simple and that's why they call me The Simplifier."

104 "If we had a free will we would simply choose to be completely happy and completely good all of the time."

105 "Life is like a movie, and we are the lead role and the observer both at the same time."

106 * "Free Will is not needed for change to occur in our universe or for humans. Change happens without free will. Energy automatically transfers and changes form and is never lost."

107 "Overcoming the illusion of free will enables us to be more understanding and compassionate towards ourselves and fellow human beings."

108 "Why professors don't refute free will at our colleges and universities is a real mystery. They all can't be that dumb."

109 "In Buddhism the concept of no personal self describes why free will is impossible."

110 "If we had a free will, we could choose our thoughts and feelings anytime we wanted."

111 "A causal will perspective encourages humility."

112 "Forgiveness would be far easier under a causal will perspective."

113 "We are predetermined to get things right, and be rewarded, and get things wrong, and be punished. How'd we screw up this free will thing so badly? Easy -- the media promotes free will every chance it can to sell news to us. Sensationalism, heroes and villains sell newspapers. The causal will life does not. The greatest ally to free will is the news media. Having

---

* Please see my book "Enlightenment Through Entitlement" to learn much more about why we (human beings) have no choice (no free will) but to seek a perceived fair exchange of our precious human energy in all our affairs.

heroes and villains, good and evil, simply sells more papers and garners better ratings."

114 "Such things as influence, genetics, and the power of suggestion equal conditioning. All kinds of factors and pressures contribute to a decision being made or not being made."

115 "While we can change our thoughts, attitudes and mood, we can't do this at will. Even when we do, it is because we have been predetermined to do so."

116 "If everything has a cause (and you knew what it was), and to understand the causal nature of the will, keep asking 'what's the cause of that?' in order to get to the bottom of things. You will soon find the answer lies in reverse infinity and that the fundamental buck stops with no one. No one ever is truly and fundamentally to blame."

117 "We may sometimes choose to endure some pain now for greater pleasure later."

118 "Because of our sub/unconscious, we can never assert with confidence what all the causes are in making a decision."

119 "Two people make exactly opposite moral decisions. Keep asking them who taught them what, where, and why and you'll soon understand that neither had nor has a free will."

120 "Neuroscientists are increasingly describing our behavior as the result of a chain of cause and effect, in which one physical brain state or pattern of neural activity leads to the next, culminating in a particular action or decision."

121 "Since there is an irrefutable chain or series of events that lead up to all decision making or action (some conscious, some sub/ unconscious), the conscious, first causing self seems to be as much fiction as a Star Wars movie."

122 "All the real action is occurring at the level of synapses and neurotransmitters—making our world one hundred percent causal."

123 "There are no such things as accidents or coincidences. Everything that happens has an underlying mathematical calculation or cause or causes. It is because there are way too many variables to calculate that many things appear to be accidental or coincidental."

124 "A random ball generator is a misnomer. It is not random at all. It is simply a very complex and long mathematical formula."

125 "Would it be the end of the world if people lost their belief in free will? Most likely not. People adapt and overcome."

126 "You are nothing but a pack of neurons. Your sense of free will a mere illusion, however persistent. It's like the grand mirage in the desert of reality. The people are all so very thirsty."

127 "A person with free will would somehow magically be able to override all the genetic and environmental factors that the person had encountered in his or her lifetime. I'd like to know how this is possible."

128 "A belief in free will contradicts the known fact that the universe and everything that makes up the universe is governed by lawful principles of math and science. People are a part of the universe, not outside the universe."

129 "Our sense of free will is deeply ingrained. We will need to invent a new syntax and vocabulary to uningrain it. See I just made up a new word. We're off to a good start."

130 "Playing off of the quote above, the belief in free will seems to be the default setting for most people. We really need to undefault that setting so that the people of tomorrow will be able live a life based on truth and reality.

131 "Truth and reality has a much better chance of sanity than lies and illusions."

132 "Just because your future life trajectory is unpredictable does not mean everything is not predetermined. There are simply too many variables. This makes life without free will just as exciting as life with free will. The only difference is the former is realistic and the latter total illusion."

133 "Social order would not break down in the unfree will futuristic scenario. People will not be allowed to break the law. The pragmatic, conventional, useful, and logistical system of justice will remain intact. Criminals will just be looked at as poorly programmed computers and not stigmatized as evil. This will be a fundamental leap of consciousness for all of mankind."

134 "I have a big problem with the word free in the context of 'free will.' The words 'free will' put together are quite confusing,

but I don't think it's the word will causing the problem. How about the following phrase: 'independent of my genes and anything that has ever happen to me' will."

135 "When goods things happen to people they like to take credit for it. When bad things happen they like to blame God. People are free will flip-floppers and tend to do so whenever and wherever possible in order to make themselves feel as best they can about themselves in any given situation."

136 "The universe has been in collusion (up until now) to have us believe in free will. I'm afraid this whole believing in free will thing has now got people in a deep sleep or hypnotic trance. We might be able to snap some people out of it for a little while, but then as soon as the issue is dropped, back to sleep they will go. We need the people to simply wake up and stay awake."

137 "The challenge before us is daunting, but not impossible. The question now is not if or when the free will illusion bubble will burst but how. How do we teach and implement a whole new way of thinking? Will there be "unfree will or causal will" commercials on television during The Superbowl? If so—who will pay for that?

138 "He did X because neuron Y fired and neurotransmitter Z was released. Another way of saying this would be he did X because he believed Y and desired Z."

139 "All mental states including belief and desire have neurobiological underpinnings. Once this concept gets illuminated, the biological basis for refuting free will becomes more convincing."

140 "We are living in the theater of the absurd, tragic, awkward, and hilarious. We are watching a play that we are starring in. A better understanding of how the brain works will be the final act in the 'Free Will' Show we are currently watching. The final act will be about how brain mechanisms work. We will then understand such things as how the brain processes desire(s), weighs options, and makes decisions based on our built up preferences. The final chapter to the story of the reasons why we act one way rather than another will eventually be told in the brain."

141 "The *feeling* of controlling one's own destiny is what people currently prefer to than the *feeling* of knowing the truth. People are simply intoxicated with the *feeling* of free will. Once they realize they've had too much to drink and that drinking too much is bad for them, will they finally sober up and understand reality as it actually is."

142 "Those claiming that causality does not rule the universe will have to explain how something could come about without it having been caused."

143 "We pray to God and hope for good outcomes from a realization that we do not have free wills. Saying things like 'It's in God's hands' and 'I had no choice in the matter' are constant reminders of the lack of free will."

144 "We treat very young children with more understanding because we don't view them as having a free will. We need to treat adults the same way. Adults are just older children still without free will."

145 *"Understanding a universe compelled justice system in the time and society you live in prohibits most people from simply doing whatever they want whenever they want. Actions will always have consequences with or without believing in free will. This is because "a perceived fair exchange of human energy" is always at stake.

146 *"The optimization imperative is a mandate from the universe which compels all of us to have no choice but to seek out perceived fair exchanges of our finite and precious human energy."

147 "Each soul has no choice but to **play the role** of being responsible for its universe compelled pragmatic karma. The casting director was a force many people call God."

148 "No one can serve The Lord without humility. The man who thinks he has a free will or has a self-willed mind and is also serving The Lord hasn't a clue about reality. It's that simple."

---

* Please see my book "Enlightenment Through Entitlement" to learn much more about why we (human beings) have no choice (no free will) but to seek a perceived fair exchange of our precious human energy in all our affairs.

149 "Most people are free will flip floppers. They love to take credit when things go well. They feel they deserve medals and raises etc. When things go wrong however, they love to blame other people or God. Free will flip flopping or double talk hypocrisy is an out of control menace to society that needs to be set straight. It's one or the other. You either have free will all the time or you don't have it all of the time. People love to use free will or lack of it at their convenience. They say they have free will under certain circumstances, but then don't have it under others. What's that all about?"

150 "You are in a play, playing a role."

The Holy Bible: No Free Will. Amen.

Book Seventeen by The Unconscious

The Book of

The Unconscious

Chapter One

"I woke up this morning and suddenly and seemingly out of nowhere I vowed to change my conditioning. There was an unconscious cause for that."

—The Unconscious

WHY am I writing this teaching in this book? I really have no idea but I know there must be a cause for it somewhere because everything has a cause. Whether or not it's unconscious or subconscious is just semantics and splitting hairs on what those two words mean.

    2 All I know is that I am not fully conscious or aware of what all the reasons and causes are to why I am writing this at this exact moment in time. Do I want to be understood? Do I want to make money? Do I want to be liked? Do I want to use this book, The Holy Bible: No Free Will, as a way to connect to people? Do I want to feel as though I accomplished something worthwhile? Do I want to seek the truth? Do I want people

to respect me? Do I want to try and make a difference in the world? Is it all of the above and then some? Probably but I'll never know for sure.

3. Definition of the subconscious or unconscious:

The sub/unconscious mind (often simply called the unconscious) is all the processes of the mind which are not available to consciousness. The term unconscious mind was coined by the 18th century German romantic philosopher Friedrich Schelling and later introduced into English by the poet and essayist Samuel Taylor Coleridge.

4. The concept gained prominence due to the influence of Austrian neurologist Sigmund Freud. Unconscious phenomena have been held to include repressed feelings, automatic skills, unacknowledged perceptions, thoughts, habits and automatic reactions, complexes, hidden phobias and desires. Within psychoanalysis the cognitive processes of the unconscious are considered to manifest in dreams in a symbolical form.

5. Thus the unconscious mind can be seen as the source of dreams and automatic thoughts (those that appear without any apparent cause), the repository of forgotten memories (that may still be accessible to consciousness at some later time), and the locus of implicit knowledge (i.e. all of the things that we have learned so well that we do them without thinking).

6. In everyday speech and in popular writing, however, the term subconscious mind is often used interchangeably with the term unconscious mind. For the purposes of this teaching I will stick with the term unconscious to mean both the subconscious and unconscious. The unconscious mind can be thought of as a repository for socially unacceptable ideas, wishes or desires, traumatic memories, and painful emotions put out of the conscious mind by the mechanism of psychological repression.

7. However, the contents do not necessarily have to be solely negative. In the psychoanalytic view, the unconscious is a force that can only be recognized by its effects—it expresses itself in the symptom.

8   Unconscious thoughts are not directly accessible to ordinary introspection, but are supposed to be capable of being "tapped" and "interpreted" by special methods and techniques such as meditation, random association, dream analysis, and verbal slips (commonly known as a Freudian slip), examined and conducted during psychoanalysis.
9   What can I say about the unconscious other than the fact that we are not aware of what's in it -- for it is unconscious.

"Unconsciously, subconsciously, semi—consciously, or consciously the universe compels people do expect others to 'live up to their side of the bargain' or 'keep up their end of the deal.' 'A deal is a deal' people often say. It appears that the pragmatic pursuit of a *perceived fair exchange of human energy is the default setting for any level of consciousness."

—The Unconscious

10 Everyone can relate to the fact that we can only have one thought at a time. Therefore, every thought we have ever had and every feeling we have ever had gets relegated to this big storage center of all our experiences in the unconscious.
11 People often do not know why they do what they do, yet are driven to do something. Most people do in fact have un/subconscious goals. Therefore, it is safe to say, that many criminals who commit heinous acts of crimes and violence haven't a clue why they committed these terrible acts. They can guess at what their true motives were, but in reality they don't have a clue.
12 We are only conscious (not conscious control, but more like a witness or simply just aware) of a tiny fraction of all the information we have ever received in life (tip of the iceberg). Most of our life is in our un/subconscious. By definition, we cannot be conscious of our un/subconscious.

---

* learn this concept in my book "Enlightenment Through Entitlement"

13 Yes we may have predispositions to certain moods if certain external events happen, but neither philosopher, theologian, neuro - scientist, nor physicist, will ever be able to fully explain why our brain states change the way they do. All we know at this point is that everything has a cause. It might be better to say it this way: "Everything has an unconscious cause."

The Holy Bible: No Free Will. Amen.

Chapter Two

EACH morning I wake up and have two packets of oatmeal. Today I had three. I have no idea why.

2. The teachings of this newer testament, The Holy Bible: No Free Will, has a very clear theory on what is going on here. The claim that we have causal wills does in fact make perfect sense, but causal to do what exactly?

3. This new kind of Bible claims that the unconscious (the unfree will) is always compelled by the universe to pragmatically pursue situations in which there is a *"perceived fair exchange" of human energy (meaning to seek more overall life satisfaction via fairness). Is this correct? Who the hell knows?

4. Sounds good to me, but if I'm only conscious of a tiny fraction of my life's history, there is no way to know for sure why I do anything. All we have left is a hypothesis or theory. The best guess scenario of why humans do what they do (chase perceived greater life satisfaction via "fair" *exchanges of human energy) is the best we can do at this time. Perceived fairness gives us great satisfaction because there is no guilt and no resentment. We desire to get exactly what we feel entitled to.

5. Every day when I leave for work, I take my cell phone with me. Last week I simply left without it. I have no idea why. I need my cell phone desperately each day for business reasons, yet I've noticed that about four times a year I simply leave home without it.

6. The last fourteen years that I've owned a cell phone, I have noticed that there is a slight pattern—I simply forget my cell phone about four times a year. There is no rhyme or reason that I can think of as to why I do this, but I do. I simply walk out the door without it and I don't know why.

7. If people, including myself, more often than not have no idea why they do what they do, how in the world could free will exist? How can human beings have a free will when the unconscious never sleeps and is more often than not running the show?

---

* learn this concept in my book "Enlightenment Through Entitlement"

8   Do not underestimate the power of the unconscious in refuting free will. Freud popularized the idea many years ago that the unconscious is the captain of the ship and it still stands true to this very day. The fact that the unconscious is in charge is yet another reason that makes free will impossible (like you needed another).

9   People often "surprise themselves." Just last month I was playing basketball. I play in a league that plays almost every week. I have been playing for about five years now. In these last five years I have averaged about six points per game. I focus mostly on good defense and rebounding.

10 My outside shot is lousy and I don't have any confidence in my inside game. I also have no idea how to drive the lane. I also play with guys who are fifteen years younger than I am, and I tire easily.

11 I am often gasping for air while they are still at full speed. I know my game (so I thought) and play within my abilities. I know my role and play into my strengths and away from my weaknesses. I have only tried at most five "3 pointers" in the last five years and I actually made one of them.

12 A month ago, I was unstoppable. I scored twenty five points (by far my all-time high). I made four "3 pointers" out of six attempts. I was "unconscious." I was in some sort of "zone." After that particular game I went back to scoring my usual six points (making layups after offensive rebounds). I have no idea what came over me that night I scored twenty five. I slept just as well, ate just as well, and had the same type of day at work.

13 What caused me to suddenly make twenty five points? Is that "free will?" If that is—why can't I freely choose to do it again? I've played four more times since that game and I can't seem to get more than four or six points no matter what I tell my mind to do. Why can't I just choose to do it again?

14 The night I scored all those points something did in fact come over me and I felt out of control (and I didn't get tired either—which never happens). How can that be "free will" when I felt out of control? Is this how crimes and murders happen? Someone just snaps and gets out of control for no apparent reason?

15 How can it be "free will" when I can't simply choose to do it again? Why was I so "out of character" that night? I don't know, will never know. If I knew, I'd obviously want to do it again . . . and again . . . and again. Something mysterious came over me.
16 Maybe it was a full moon? Maybe I was hit by cosmic rays that day? Maybe there was a cute girl in the stands? Maybe the "stars were aligned" in a certain way (people sometimes actually say this)? Maybe it was a song I heard that day? I have no idea what came over me.
17 Many people have conscious goals. But then they "self-sabotage" themselves. Why would someone "self-sabotage" him/herself? Why would someone who works at a place where drinking on the job is forbidden get caught drinking on the job the day before he got promoted (and hence lose the promotion).
18 His proclaimed and conscious goal (of five years mind you) was a promotion to manager. He had never drank alcohol previously while on the job in the last five years that he was employed there. Why the day before? What is going on here with self- sabotage?

"People have sub/unconscious goals. I have no idea why this chapter is ending now, but I'm sure there's an unconscious/subconscious cause for it."

—The Unconscious

"Just because you don't consciously know what the cause is, doesn't mean the cause doesn't exist. The cause exists and doesn't care if you are aware of it or not."

—The Unconscious

"People mistakenly believe they have free will because they make what they believe to be uncaused choices or decisions. This gives people the **illusory feeling** of free will. The truth of the matter is that everything has a cause, and more often than not, that cause is in the sub/unconscious."

—The Unconscious

- There are causes in the environment that people are unaware of causing their decision making. For example—a certain type of music in a restaurant causes the patron to order a certain type of wine (from a certain country). When asked why they chose that particular type of wine, the customer will say "it tastes better."
- For more information about this topic read "Subliminal: How Your Unconscious Mind Rules Your Behavior" by Leonard Mlodinow

The Holy Bible: No Free Will. Amen.

Book Eighteen by The Vindicator

The Book of

Vindication

Chapter One

HOW we are vindicated and why having . . .

<u>a causal will creates</u>

<u>a better world.</u>

If people can come to the truth about their lack of control over how others feel about them, how others treat them, how we feel about ourselves, then people's severe guilt, severe blame, severe resentment, and overall severe acrimony (and all other severe and intense negative emotions) will instantly become modified. Severe toxic guilt, blame, acrimony and resentment go hand and hand with the belief that human beings have a free will.

2. We all need to be able to feel healthy guilt or "acting as if" we have free will guilt otherwise known as "pragmatic or practical guilt." This pragmatic guilt, blame, or resentment comes from

the feeling of actual wrongdoing (internal moral code). But "severe free will" toxic guilt is not good for anyone. Not good for you, not good for me, and most importantly not good for society. You can move beyond "severe free will" toxic guilt by understanding that free will is an illusion and modify all emotions to simply a more modified and simply useful and pragmatic level.

3 * the "free will" belief that you can control others feelings and behavior by doing things "right" --> leads to . . .

* leads to self-judgment to control your own behavior to get yourself to do it "right" --> leads to . . .

* which leads to severe emotional and toxic guilt (blame or resentment).

The way out of severe emotional and toxic guilt is to simply understand that free will is an illusion and doesn't exist on the fundamental level:

4 * full acceptance of your lack of control over others feelings and behavior --> leads to . . .

* which leads to a lessening of self-judgment --> leads to . . .

* which leads to a lessening of severe, intense, and toxic guilt, blame, and resentment.

5 With practice, you can completely eliminate your severe and toxic guilt (and all other severe negative emotions). Practice makes progress and it takes practice, conditioning, and training to constantly remind oneself of the very harmful consequences of believing that humans have "free will." The more you practice your belief that there is no free will, the more progress you will make in freeing yourself from such severe and toxic emotions such as hate and envy.

6 After years of research on subjects ranging from toddlers to sailors to Tibetan monks, neuroscientists are now increasingly concluding that causal brain activity underlie all human emotionality.

> "There are no mistakes, just chances we've taken based on causality."
>
> —The Vindicator

7. The formation of our decision making is a causal process. Hence our preferences and our decisions are caused. Others may believe it were possible for us to make other decisions.
8. They tell us "you could have done this or that." "Should have done this or that." Or if you "would have only" done this or that.
9. Other people are not you. They are mere outsiders and not privy to what your unique causal antecedents make you, you. They are completely ignorant of your entire decision-making process. If they were you, atom for atom, then they would have done what you did. But they are not.
10. For other people to claim that we could have decided and done otherwise is completely incoherent. These people seek to impose their internal private life paradigms or world view upon yours. It is completely unwarranted for one human being to tell another human being what they could have done differently or how they could have behaved otherwise. It's ok to admonish someone in order to modify and change their behavior for the next time, but it is not ok to tell someone how they could have done otherwise in the past.
11. Other people do not share your options (or lack of options). They do not share your modus operandi, your genetics, or your past experiences. In short, they have no idea what it's like to be you. Only you do.

> "What we choose to do is never out of 'free choice' but was always out of necessity. All your past mistakes are hereby vindicated."
>
> —The Vindicator

12. The belief in free will no longer serves us. In our sports crazed culture it is like a completely out of date stadium. Take for example a baseball team that plays in a climate where it is always

way too hot, or rains on and off almost every day? The Florida Marlins come to mind. Why would this team not play in a retractable air conditioned dome?

13. The answer would be—the technology was not yet invented yet and/or it didn't make economic sense. The widespread knowledge of how to build such a facility and the ability to afford it were not yet options for this baseball team -- until now that is.

14. But now in the 2020s, they know the truth about the technology being available AND the knowledge of how to afford it. So why would they stick to something that no longer serves them logically or financially? The answer is -- they wouldn't and they didn't.

15. The Florida Marlins now The Miami Marlins understood what was old and antiquated and what no longer served them. When they found a better option they understood it and then built it. They simply discarded the old (which no longer served them) and brought in the new (which now makes more logical sense and does serve them).

16. So the belief in free will is like an old antiquated stadium that no longer serves mankind. It's time we all built ourselves a nice new stadium. We now know how to build it and we can afford it. We also know how to name it.

17. Welcome to the "Causal Will" retractable air conditioned dome. This is our new stadium. It suits us now. It feels current and modern. It simply makes more sense.

"When you give up the belief in free will, you will also give up a life of animosity and acrimony."

—The Vindicator

18. I had a problem. I didn't know what to do. I had three choices A, B or C. I spoke to 15 people (most of them highly paid advisers and "experts"). All 15 people advised me to pick A or B. I thanked them for their advice and picked C anyway.

"Everything that happens is followed by something else which depends on it by causal necessity. Likewise, everything that occurs is preceded by something with which it is causally connected. Nothing can exist or has come into existence in the entire universe without a cause."

—The Vindicator

19. As with breaking any addiction, it's easier to ride with the short term feel good than try to do what's best in the long run. We must acknowledge the reality of what we are as a species for that is our grand purpose for being here at all. We must all come together and understand that free will is a grand hoax on humanity.
20. We must acknowledge the science, and the cold hard facts that free will is just a feeling, and just an illusion. We can use this knowledge to make our lives, our society, and our personal interactions better. Soon we will do away with poisonous fundamental blame.
21. Our so called "free will" society simply hasn't worked out so well. Depression and misery are everywhere. Why don't we try to get to the root of our problems? Why not get a firm grip on what brings about all the harm (the causes) and learn how to prevent them. The only way to do this is to look at human beings for what they actually are and to strip them of this antiquated nonsense of free will. Then we can address all the antecedents that create the causal conduct we as a society disapprove of.
22. Human beings are a part of nature and subject to all natural laws. The most important natural and psychological law is that human beings have no choice but to always go in the direction of greater satisfaction (no free will).

"Nothing is voluntary. Everything by necessity."

—The Vindicator

- The word 'will' has many definitions. In the context of "free will" it means the ability to make decisions. Human beings make decisions all the time and there is no refuting that. Yes human beings have a will, it just isn't 'free' will.
- Once you fully exonerate yourself and others for all the silly and stupid mistakes that were made will you ironically truly be free. Once you fully understand that human wills are causal and compelled by the entirety of the universe, can you truly forgive yourself and others. From this day forward no matter what happens to you please remember everything is God willed and meant to be exactly as it is. Every second of your life is God's will.

"You can choose your preferences, you just can't choose what you prefer."

"You can choose your desires, you just can't choose what you desire."

"You can infer meaning, you just can't choose what meaning you infer."

—The Vindicator

The Holy Bible: No Free Will. Amen.

Chapter Two

*ON August 1, 1966, Charles Whitman murdered his mother and his wife before traveling to the campus of the University of Texas, climbing inside the tower, and killing fourteen others. He was dubbed the infamous UT sniper, but his story involves much more than Marine Corps training and a proclivity for violence. In fact, Whitman complained of headaches and an altered mental state in the days and weeks leading up to the killings. His own suicide note read that "I do not really understand myself these days. I am supposed to be an average reasonable and intelligent young man. However, lately (I cannot recall when it started) I have been a victim of many unusual and irrational thoughts."

> 2 Whitman knew that something was wrong. His note further reads, "After my death I wish that an autopsy would be performed on me to see if there is any visible physical disorder." And indeed there was. Whitman was found to have a glioblastoma, a type of brain tumor, pressing against regions of the brain thought to be responsible for the regulation of strong emotions.

"The Truth Sells Itself."

—The Vindicator

"No matter how heinous, vicious, and cruel the crime that we committed may be, in the eyes of The Lord God, the universe, the cosmos etc., we are all fundamentally innocent."

—The Vindicator

"There is no judgment day forthcoming in which some of us go to heaven, while others go to hell. The Lord, God cannot judge a man for his will is not free."

—The Vindicator

"You have no choice but to live life in your own peculiar way."

—The Vindicator

*3 A British man who claims to have "woken up gay" after a gym accident led him to suffer a stroke is speaking out about his experience to the BBC.
4   Kris Birch, who works as a hairdresser, was known to his Welsh friends and family as a rugby-loving jock prior to the stroke. But the 26-year-old Birch says he realized his personality had completely changed as he was recovering. His story caused a sensation late last year after being reported by the Daily Mail among other publications.
5   At the time, Birch told the Daily Mirror that his most profound discovery came while he was watching a TV program featuring a handsome actor. "I felt my stomach flutter and the same feelings I used to have for pretty girls came across me," said Birch, who also added he was no longer interested in sports and had little in common with old friends. "I had never felt like that about a man before but I knew immediately what the feeling was. I fancied him."
6   Hmm. Perhaps this will be solid proof that your sexual orientation is clearly brain-wiring. I wouldn't doubt it. It's the same as those who are wired to be left handed, wired to be sensitive, or wired to be flexible. The brain has many things that make it up, so this, comes as no surprise.

"Whatever is meant to be is meant to be. Say goodbye to all the silly and stupid mistakes you made. You and I are hereby vindicated. We had no choice, have no choice, and will have no choice in whatever happens to us going forward. It's all about cause and effect conditioning (classical or operant etc.), how we were raised, and our genetics. It's all about having no choice but to go towards pleasure and away from pain."

—The Vindicator

*The source of these articles was taken from an article written on the home page of the AOL news section (from the internet).

"Whether or not one believes in heaven and hell, God, religion, scientology, enlightenment, or reincarnation is insignificant to me. All that matters to me is whether or not you believe you have a free will. Whatever you believe in, you were conditioned to believe it. If you believe you have a free will, then you were conditioned to believe that. Same is true for people who do not believe in free will.

—Nick Vale

"The point and theory that overrides all belief systems and thought patterns is simple: you have no choice but to believe what you believe because you perceive **it feels best** for you to believe it."

—Nick Vale

"The cat's out of the bag now about this whole free will being an illusion thing. It's about time."

—Nick Vale

"I often can't do what I want to do and can't stop doing what I don't want to do."

—Everyone Can Say This

The Holy Bible: No Free Will. Amen.

Book Nineteen by The Harmer

The Book of

Why Free Will is Bad for Society

The below is a summary of an article called:

The Surprising Link Between Homicide Rates and the Belief in Free Will

New research suggests we believe that people have choices because we want to see some of them get punished.

In a new study which was published in Journal of Personality and Social Psychology shows in many different ways how and why the belief in free will is bad for society. The hypothesis of the study as stated by the authors was to "propose that the pervasive belief in free will partially flows from a desire for moral responsibility in order to justify punishing others for their anti-social behaviors. Therefore, when there is a desire to punish, people should be motivated to believe in free will."

> 2 In other words, people enjoy being on what one could call the "moral superiority thrill ride." This means that when people believe in free will, they also open up the door to feeling morally superior to another. This is one of the many reasons people thoroughly enjoy their nonsensical belief in free will.

When they see someone else do something wrong (the bad guy), and they believe that the wrong doing was freely willed, it automatically makes the non-wrong doing person (the good guy) feel better about themselves and in a sense morally superior. This is what makes people enjoy telling other people that a certain "person is crazy and evil and will spend the rest of eternity rotting in hell."

3. It's a classic case of it makes me feel better to see someone else do something wrong because clearly they could have used their free will and not done wrong. They made a bad free choice (free will) and they should suffer for this bad free choice (free will). Clearly, they could have done otherwise.

4. A team of authors from several universities (the University of California-Irvine, Yale University, and two others) have put the above thesis to the experimental test.

5. The study then proceeds to back up its hypothesis in five separate experiments. In one of the experiments, 277 students in an undergraduate psychology course got a surprise email from their professor two days after they had taken their midterm exam. The email they received said one of three things: 1) that a student had been caught cheating on the exam, and had been punished; 2) that someone had cheated on the exam (because a cheat sheet was found in the exam room) but the perpetrator had not yet been identified or punished; or 3) that an undescribed "activity" would be taking place in the next class (the "control" group). Then, all the students were asked to complete a questionnaire asking their level of agreement with statements like "criminals are totally responsible for the bad things they do" and "strength of mind can always overcome the body's desires."

6. Sure enough, the students who had read the emails about cheating (emails one or two) showed a stronger belief in the existence of free will than the students who had received the control email (email three).

7. Three other experiments reported in the paper reached a similar conclusion using a variety of different designs and methodologies. Finally, to top it all off, the researchers conducted an independent analysis of real-world statistics that are relevant to the question at hand.

8 The study authors proceeded to look for a relationship between a country's average belief in free will and homicide rates in that country, hypothesizing that more crime-ridden places would also tend to believe more strongly in free will, presumably out of a desire to see criminals punished.

9 They were able to obtain adequate data for 74 countries. And sure enough, for these countries there was a marked relationship between homicide rates and belief in free will. For instance, countries like Venezuela, Columbia, and Guatemala—which have very high homicide rates (Venezuela's was about 45 homicides per 100,000 people in 2010) —also have citizens who believe strongly in free will.

10 It is therefore safe to deduce that the following three societal problems are made worse by the belief in free will (and hence why free will is bad for society).

11 #1 That if the belief in free will is strongly present, people will be more likely to deeply, fundamentally, and truly blame another for their actions (as opposed to just pragmatically blame them for their actions). This feeling of deep hate towards another human being can only increase feelings of homicidal rage (want to see another suffer and be punished). Deduction: More Homicides. Result - Bad for Society.

12 #2 Therefore, it also follows that the belief in free will is also responsible for deeply, fundamentally, and truly blaming oneself for one's actions. This feeling of deep hate towards oneself can only increase feelings of suicidal rage (want to see ourselves suffer and be punished). Deduction: More Suicides. Result - Bad for Society.

13 #3 George Ortega's book entitled Free Will: Its Refutation, Societal Cost and Role in Climate Change Denial explains why and how the belief in free will is actually causing people to deny climate change. Deduction: Free Will Belief Causes Climate Change Denial. Result - Bad for Society.

14 Please note: In George Ortega's book he cites nine more studies published in research journals that suggest attributing blame correlates with people having . . . .

*1 more aggression and violent seeking of revenge and retribution
*2 less forgiveness

*3 more interpersonl conflict
*4 less compassion
*5 less charity
*6 more anger towards others
*7 more anxiety and depression
*8 more arrogance and belittling of others
*9 more self -blame and guilt

*1 Folger and Baron, 1996; Wickens, Wiesenthal, Flora and Flett, 2011
*2 Bradfield and Aquino, 1999; Meneses and Greenberg, 2011
*3 Cashmore and Parkinson, 2011; DeBoard-Lucas, Fosco, Raynor, and Grych, 2010; Meneses and Greenberg
*4 Decety, Echols and Correll, 2010; Zucker and Weiner, 1993
*5 Campbell, Carr and MacLachlan, 2001; Carr and MacLachlan, 1998; Cheung and Chan, 2000
*6 Csibi and Csibi, 2011; Decety, Echols and Correll; Martinko and Zellars, 1998; Meneses and Greenberg
*7 Csibi and Csibi; DeBoard-Lucas, Fosco, Raynor, and Grych; Fourie, Rauch, Morgan, Ellis, Jordaan and Thomas, 2011; O'Connor, Kotze and Wright, 2011; Raskauskas, 2010
*8 Decety, Echols and Correll; Miceli and Castelfranchi, 2011; O'Connor, Kotze and Wright.
*9 Csibi and Csibi; Fourie, Rauch, Morgan, Ellis, Jordaan and Thomas; de Guzman et.al., 2010 Ni-colle, Bach, Frith and Dolan, 2011; O'Connor, Kotze and Wright

It is then deduced from all these studies above that the stronger the belief in free will the more likely such things as homicide, suicide, and climate change denial will occur.

The Holy Bible: No Free Will. Amen.

Book Twenty by Occam's razor

The Book of

The Law of Parsimony

1. If determinism is true, then there is no free will.
2. If indeterminism is true, then there is no free will.
3. Either determinism is true or indeterminism is true.
4. Therefore, there is no free will (from 1-3)
5. Man cannot be a Self-Causer or First Causer. Why is this true?

   a) An Agent (a human being called S), S, has free will if and only if, with respect to at least one choice . . .
   b) S could have done otherwise than S's choice . . . therefore . . .
   c) S's choice is ultimately up to S or within S's full control. This would mean . . . S could be a self - causer or first causer . . . therefore . . .

      i) S would not have a past history of preferences built up inside him or
      ii) her from either genetics, past experiences (conditioning), or some combination of both (nature and/or nurture). That would mean . . .
      iii) With all preferences erased, all choices would appear exactly equal (50/50). Hence S would have no preferences.

iv) Therefore: S would not know what to choose for all of eternity. S would be frozen solid forever with indecision.
v) Therefore if S is not frozen solid with indecision for all of eternity S must have a preference. It does not matter if S knows or knows not the cause or origin of his or her preference. All S has to know is that a decision must be made. Note: S may choose to not make a choice (preference) which is a choice (preference).
vi) Therefore it is deduced: S's choice (preference) is part of a causal chain stretching back before S's birth since S did not give birth to him/herself.
vii) S was not the cause of him/herself coming into existence. S's parents were the cause of S's birth.
viii) Therefore: S's choice (preference) was not freely willed. It was part of a causal chain that S did not originate. S was not the originator of his existence.
ix) Therefore: S does not have free will.

The Holy Bible: No Free Will. Amen.

Book Twenty One: by Nick Vale

The Book of
Epilogue

Epilogue:

The internet and cell phones have from my perspective sped up growing up to such a degree, that the problem of western societies in particular is that we no longer have to fight to just exist. We have more food than we need and warm shelter. Existence has become so easy, that the only thing left to do on planet earth is to make the whole damn thing into a silly game.

2. In other words, by making life into just a silly game, we can actually find some meaning and a reason to live. But what happens when the silly game becomes too stupid, boring, silly or difficult? Well then that's where our unfree will to live gets destroyed and suicide becomes a viable alternative to many of us.
3. Why play a silly stupid game if we don't like it anymore? Then we invent new needs for ourselves such as stupid social constructs to stroke our egos with. These include such things as the "best" schools to go to, the "best" jobs, the "hottest" wife, the "best" country club to belong to, the "best" hotels to stay in etc. etc. I hate to say this, but that's all we have left.

4. The need for love, a family, a perfect body, a car, a mansion, fame is really all pure stupidity if you really think about it. But that's all life is about now and it's understandable that many of us don't want to live on such a stupid planet—the "game" of life is quite ridiculous when all that is left is pleasing the ego. Then we must take into account that even if we had eternal beauty, wealth and fame (or whatever else we desire) we a) wouldn't appreciate it if we were born with it or b) would find earth even more bland and boring if we knew we always would have it.
5. So were screwed either way because if we had all we desired forever and forever life would be even more boring, but on the other hand if we don't have it—then life becomes a silly and stupid game to attain such social constructs and ego pleasers.
6. Admittedly, it is very hard or near impossible to penetrate through this sludge of social depravity since it has set in hard over the years. Prior generations have made it a way of life to want to "get ahead," and people have actually acquired the convenient skill of blocking off ideas, concepts, and suggestions that do not appeal to them (such as free will being an illusion). The shallowness of a "well adjusted" human being is downright frightful. If you were to point out the shallowness to a "well adjusted" human's existence, they would most likely tell you or snap at you "why are you so deep?"
7. The ability to block pure logic (that man's will is not free) and consequently build a false or real happiness based on the current faulty model is simply not spiritually or fundamentally correct. Why is everyone living in the grand illusion that is free will? If everyone has it so wrong then what is the answer to why we exist?
8. The answer has to be found in wanting to know the truth about things.
9. You should not be hated, made to feel ashamed or guilty for any so-called psychological disorder. This is true because everyone has his or her own unique and personal way to so-called "happiness" or a more peaceful state of mind. All you have to say to yourself is the following: "I know it's not everyone's path, but it is mine."
10. I find all my beauty in this world in the truth that free will is an illusion.

11 I prefer truths to lies every time because that's the only real beauty in this world that is left.
12 Please just let me know the truth about things for it is the only truly meaningful endeavor that remains. That's all I ask.
13 I believe the only true shame that should be felt on this earth is a very intense shame that we ALL SHOULD FEEL at what we are as a species up until this point (but we cannot blame ourselves because our wills are not free).
14 The universe has simply duped us all by this free will thing and it simply needs to be set straight once and for all. The time is now and that is crystal clear.
15 Many of us who believe that free will is an illusion feel that no matter how many ways we phrase and rephrase what we are saying, we feel like we are talking to a brick wall.
16 This is then usually followed by a weak sense of futility. Other times a strong sense of futility sets in. Either way a sense of futility sets in and then comes the "why does anything really matter?" feeling.
17 The truth matters. It just does. Our species needs to get this free will thing corrected once and for one reason and one reason only. It's simply the truth about reality.
18 It's just not spiritually correct to believe in free will.
19 What I am trying to say is that life for these newer generations seems to not matter much, if at all. The only possible way it could matter is to get to the truth of things since all other avenues to happiness now appear to be closed off. The last great truth to be discovered is that free will is just an illusion.
20 This I feel, will help mankind greatly as self—blame will soon cease to exist. When this begins to happen, people will in fact become a little happier.
21 Take away free will, you take away self—blame. Once you take away self—blame, you basically instantly stop 99% of all suicides. This is because self—hatred or self—blame is simply not possible in a non-free will based mindset.
22 Once people become armed with the knowledge that their messed up lives were not and will not be their fault, will people start to once again begin to actually enjoy themselves. The pressure on all of us to "have great lives" will finally be off.

23 Once you internalize the concept that free will is just an illusion, will you begin to truly smile again. This is because you will be living in the truth that none of this was your fault.

"Living a life in a lie or an illusion just doesn't feel right. The truth about all of us having zero free will, will ironically set us all 'free.'"

—Nick Vale

24 Things and people just come here and exist the way they are and fated to be so and that's just the way it is.
25 As far as I can tell, the only real purpose of humanity is to now finally get this free will thing straighten out.
26 The pursuit of truth is the only real purpose of being a human being. What else could it be?
27 You see—you just can't lose once you understand that free will is just an illusion and that you are always doing the best you can (Optimization Imperative).

"There is always an 'invisible gun to your head' as everything you do is the only thing you can be doing (or could have done) based on everything that has happen to you before."

—Nick Vale

"Yes you are pragmatically responsible for your karma (cause and effect). But ultimately and fundamentally you are not responsible for your karma (cause and effect)."

—Nick Vale

"A new legal vocabulary will have to be invented for the coming causal will society that now knows that free will is pure illusion. For example: in any court case the defendant will now be called the 'represented cause by the universe' or more succinctly the 'proximate cause of this situation.' In this new 'no free will' society, the word 'blame' will only be used pragmatically and will eventually lose its stigma evoking power (since everyone will now know that free will is pure illusion and fantasy). People will still be 'blamed' pragmatically (actions will still obviously have consequences freely willed or not), but only as the 'karmic representative of the unfortunate situation' or as previously stated the 'proximate causer.' Another way the court may address the guilty party is by simply saying 'you are hereby blamelessly/faultlessly responsible.'"

—Nick Vale

28 Neuroscience of free will refers to the recent neuro-scientific investigation of questions concerning free will. As it has become possible to study the living brain, researchers have begun to watch decision making processes at work.

Relevant findings include the pioneering study by Benjamin Libet and its subsequent redesigns (Chun Siong Soon for example); these studies were able to detect activity related to a decision to move, and the activity appears to be **occurring briefly before people become conscious of it.**

"Everything (including the Heisenberg Uncertainty Principle) is either causal or random and neither proves free will.

"The last quark was only discovered about 27 years ago and the Higgs Boson was just discovered in July of 2012. *New discoveries happen all the time."

"If you contend that you are a 'first causer' and a 'little God' then you wouldn't know what to do next as every option would appear just as good as any other. You would magically lose all preferences and would no longer know what you preferred in any given situation . . . somehow all your past experiences would magically be erased. Choices are never 50/50—hence no free will."

- Without free will, life just becomes a matter of 'luck' or 'unluck.' Luck or unluck by definition means you cannot control it. It just happens and you have no control over how 'lucky' or 'unlucky' your time on earth feels to you."

---

* For example: new discovery of exotic particles in 2022 include the pentaquark and tetraquark.

- The belief in 'Free' will is total and complete utter nonsense.
- We are obviously not free to choose things that simply don't occur to us.

"Our wills are simply not of our own making. Thoughts and intentions emerge from background causes which we are unaware and over which we exert no conscious control. We do not have the freedom we think we have."

—Sam Harris

"What will my next mental state be? I do not know—it just happens. Where is the freedom in that?"

—Sam Harris

"How much credit does a person deserve for not being lazy? None at all. Laziness, like diligence, is a neurological condition."

—Sam Harris

Free Will or No Free Will?—that is the question. Why can we talk about anything on this planet EXCEPT the big one? That being... when will people realize that there is no such thing as free will? www.nofreewill.info and www.nofreewill.org are good places to start. Sam Harris is spot on also with his book "free will."

I want to know why there is no public debate show about this issue. Sooner or later there will be, we have no choice.

"If I were an 'evil' other person, I'd be that 'evil' other person. Atom for Atom, Quark for Quark, Neuron for Neuron, Neutrino for Neutrino, Higgs Boson for Higgs Boson, and the same exact 'evil' soul and mind and all... I'd have that person's same exact consciousness.

With his/her exact same genetics, his/her exact same conditioning, and his/her exact same 'evil' soul. I'd be him/her in every exact and conceivable way and would've acted the same exact way in every regard possible. 'Free Will' is nowhere to be found."

—Nick Vale

"Whether or not one believes in heaven and hell, God, religion, scientology, enlightenment, or reincarnation is insignificant to me. All that matters to me is whether or not you believe you have a free will. Whatever you believe in, you were conditioned to believe it. If you believe you have a free will, then you were conditioned to believe that. Same is true for people who do not believe in free will. The point and theory that overrides all belief systems and thought patterns is simple: you have no choice but to believe what you believe because you perceive **it feels best** for you to believe it. This is the hedonic imperative which states that all human behavior goes toward pleasure and away from pain."

—Nick Vale

- I woke up this morning and suddenly and seemingly out of nowhere I vowed to change my conditioning. There was an unconscious cause for that.
- Ding dong the witch is dead. The witch is dead. The witch is dead. Ding dong the wickedest witch of all (the belief in free will) is now dead. Ding dong the witch is dead. The witch is dead. The witch is dead. Ding dong the witch is dead. This particularly wicked witch is now finally dead.
- The Holy Bible: No Free Will is one of our planet's most important new developments.

The understanding that free will is an illusion may be the most important achievement of our intelligent but wayward species.

- I often can't do what I want to do and can't stop doing what I don't want to do.
- The taboo subject of openly refuting free will is now finally no longer taboo. As of this new kind of Bible, it is now out in the open
- The pursuit of truth, is by process of elimination, the last great beautiful and noble endeavor to be truly alive for. We've simply tried everything else. We're at our wits end now and there's just

nothing else that really matters except getting to the bottom of this free will issue and finding out the truth.
- New truth is often uncomfortable. This is especially true to the holders of power the new truth threatens.

The Holy Bible: No Free Will. Amen

Book Twenty Two

The Book of

About the author, Contact the author, Dedication, Many Thanks

ABOUT THE AUTHOR

Nick Vale a.k.a. "Enel" Vale has a BBA from Emory University, an MBA in Finance from Fordham University, is a proud member of Mensa (top 2% IQ society), and is the executive producer, producer, writer, director and host of the only New York City weekly television show entirely devoted to refuting free will. The show is called "Free Will?" and is a live call in show that runs every week on Manhattan Neighborhood Network at 11pm each Wednesday for 30 minutes and has been running since September 2011. The author is also the co-host of the White Plains, NY weekly show called "Exploring the Illusion of Free Will" which is a discussion show about the illusion of free will. The author has also traveled extensively all over the world (40+ countries) and all over the USA (40+ states). The author was born in Portugal and was raised in Manhattan, New York City. He attended Trinity High School.

Contact The Author:

The author's private email is Nick1971v@aol.com. Also see www.nofreewill.info and www.nofreewill.org.

Please refrain from thanking me for writing this book for my will was not free.

I am blamelessly and faultlessly responsible for writing this book.

I am pragmatically responsible for writing this book, but not ultimately or fundamentally responsible for writing this book.

I am lucky or unlucky to have had the universe allow me to write this book.

Dedicated to and for:

Future generations who will understand man's will is not free

The Father of all Fathers and the King of all Kings (Lord God)

The Mother of all Mothers and the Queen of all Queens (Lord God)

The inventor and creator of the finite universe, the infinite universe, or the universe that is both

The universe that had a creation date

The universe that has always been here

The universe that was created and has always been here

The unfathomable, incomprehensible, inexplicable, and inconceivable first causer who created the law of causality

The universe that didn't have a first cause (was always here) and always had the law of causality embedded in it (cause and effect)

Father Time and Mother Nature

Peace of mind for all via The Holy Bible: No Free Will

Many Thanks to:

Many Thanks to Seymour Lessans for writing "Decline and Fall of All Evil: The Most Important Discovery of Our Times." As far-fetched as this book is, the amount of passion, care, and effort he took in trying to figure out what it would mean for the world to understand man's will is not free should be recognized. Many thanks to his daughter Janis Rafael for all her work in her father's effort as well. Of course it's difficult to thank either of them since they didn't actually do anything (no free will). But I have no choice but to thank them for pragmatic reasons.

Many Thanks to Gerard 't Hooft (Nobel Prize in Physics 1999) for believing that there should be a deterministic theory underlying quantum mechanics. Of course it's difficult to thank him since he didn't actually do anything (no free will). But I have no choice but to thank him for pragmatic reasons.

Many thanks to John Searle. John Searle is one of the most quoted philosophers of all time. John Searle understood how important this free will debate is. He said and I quote "overcoming the free will illusion would be a bigger revolution in our thinking than Einstein, or Copernicus, or Newton, or Galileo, or Darwin -- it would alter our whole conception of our relation with the universe." Of course it's difficult to thank him since he didn't actually do anything (no free will). But I have no choice but to thank him for pragmatic reasons.

Many thanks to Sam Harris. Sam Harris wrote a book called "Free Will" which should be recognized. His book help popularize the fact that free will is an illusion and was one of the first mainstream books to do so. Of course it's difficult to thank him since he didn't actually do anything (no free will). But I have no choice but to thank him for pragmatic reasons.

Many thanks to George Ortega for starting the "Exploring the Illusion of Free Will" Meet up in New York City. He should win the Nobel Prize for Explaining Reality (if such an award existed). Please see his website www.causalconsciousness.com. He also has written an excellent book entitled "Free Will: Its refutation, societal cost, and role in Climate Change Denial." Of course it's difficult to thank him since he didn't actually do anything (no free will). But I have no choice but to thank him for pragmatic reasons.

Many thanks to Albert Einstein and Stephen Hawking for also not believing in free will.

Of course it's difficult to thank them since they didn't actually do anything (no free will). But I have no choice but to thank them for pragmatic reasons.

The Holy Bible: No Free Will. Amen

Book Twenty-Three by Quick Summary

The Book of

Why Free Will Is Impossible

The pleasure principle is hereby proved by the fact that you probably skipped reading the whole book and simply wanted the answer as fast as possible. This is why you are reading the last book first entitled "why free will impossible" The pleasure principle states you are always doing what gives you the most amount of satisfaction available to you at the time.

    2 You have no choice but to always go towards pleasure and away from pain (doing what gives you the most amount of overall satisfaction). Yes, feeling depressed is the most amount of satisfaction available to you at the time. There must be some sort of satisfaction in being depressed unbeknownst to you (sub/unconscious). It is the lesser of two evils (or more). In short, depression and misery are not free choices. They are based on your causal history that lead up to that point in time. If you don't want to feel depressed at all then simply "snap out of it" and simply use your free will to get out of it. This is of course impossible. This is why most people must face depression and other negative emotions. They have no free choice in the matter. Surely, if people had free will, depression would not exist.

3. We cannot stop ourselves from being born. We had no choice in the matter.
4. We then have two choices. Commit suicide or live out our lives as best we can.
5. Every moment in time, every motion, from the beating heart to the slightest reflex action, from all the inner and outer movements of the body, indicates that life is never satisfied or content to remain in one identical position for always like an inanimate object, which position shall be termed death.
6. The present moment in time is (here) and the next moment in time is (there). Going to the spot (there) from (here) always has two options. You are now reading this sentence in a moment in time (here) and here are your two options: One can either remain living (there) or kill yourself (there). Either move to the next spot called (there) alive or move to the next spot called (there) dead (commit suicide).
7. Consequently, the motion of all life is any motion from (here) to (there) -- one moment in time to the next moment in time, is always a motion which you have no control over and hence man's will is not free. Every motion of life has no choice but to go in one direction and one direction only. This is the direction of greater satisfaction otherwise known as always being forced to attempt to attain more pleasure and therefore less pain. This is called The Pleasure Principle.
8. Since the motion of life always constantly moves from (here) to (there), which is an expression of dissatisfaction with the present position, it must naturally follow in the direction of greater satisfaction. This is why you "cut to the chase" and read the last book/chapter first. You had no choice but to desire a "quick summary."
9. It should now be obvious that our desire to keep living, to move off the spot of this moment (here), to the next moment (there), is determined by a masturbatory psychological law over which we have no control. We must always seek out more pleasure and greater overall satisfaction. It is therefore axiomatically impossible to purposely go towards less satisfaction.

Even if we should kill ourselves in this very next moment (there), we are choosing what we believe will give us greater satisfaction, otherwise we would not kill ourselves.

10. The truth is at any particular moment in time the motion of man's will is not free because his will must obey this natural and immutable law of the universe. Man is compelled by his nature to make choices that he prefers within the options available to him that will lead him under his present belief system to find greater satisfaction (pleasure).
11. He must always choose what he believes will be better for himself and his overall set of circumstances (all things considered). There is no choice in the matter.
12. You are doing the same exact thing right now as you "cut to the chase" and didn't want to read this book in the order it was presented to you.
13. You had no choice but to desire a "quick summary" and read the last book first.
14. For example, when mankind found that a discovery like the automobile was for his benefit in comparison to travel by horse, he was compelled to prefer it for his transportation. Just by staying alive and not committing suicide, he has always been attempting to go in the direction of greater pleasure and overall life satisfaction. The Amish people have no free choice but to still prefer horse travel because it gives them greater satisfaction. This is what feels best to them psychologically based on their culture and belief system. It is patently axiomatically impossible to knowingly go in the direction of greater life dissatisfaction.
15. If you are at this present moment in time (this exact instant) coming up with reasons about why I am so wrong about this point (maybe even shouting at this new kind of Bible), then you are in fact in this very moment in time proving me correct. You are in fact obeying this psychological and natural law of the universe. By you trying to prove me all wrong, you are by no will of your own trying to find greater satisfaction.

16. You want to prove your point so badly and have no choice in the matter because it would give you greater satisfaction to prove me all wrong otherwise commit suicide. If suicide is less preferable at this time (which I sincerely hope), then you have no choice (as long as you are staying alive) to prove me all wrong or agree with me (you have no choice but to do whatever gives you more satisfaction). So since I am quite sure that of the three options, suicide will give you the least amount of overall life satisfaction, then you have no choice but to try and prove me all wrong or agree with me. If you agree with everything I am writing here, then this is the option by default giving you the most satisfaction. Perhaps you will help join the No Free Will movement and pass this book along? Consequently, during every moment of man's existence (progress) he always did what he had to do because he had no choice. This no choice is to always go towards greater overall life satisfaction based on one's best estimation and prediction of what would bring him or her the most overall life satisfaction.

17. Regardless of how many examples you experiment with the results will always be the same because this is an immutable psychological and natural law. You simply cannot purposely choose what gives you less satisfaction. You can choose your preferences, but you cannot choose what you prefer. Your preferences are based on your genetics and conditioning. Free will is nowhere to be found.

18. From moment to moment all through life man can never move in the direction of dissatisfaction on purpose, and that his every motion, conscious or unconscious, is a natural effort to get rid of some dissatisfaction or move to some greater satisfaction. If reading this Bible of No Free Will is not the most satisfying thing you could be doing right now, then you will have no choice but to close this book and do something else. This might be true in this very moment in time as I have become quite redundant in what I am trying to explain to you. It is now quite possible that my repetitiveness is making you less satisfied than you were before when my concept was new and fresh to you.

19. Every motion of life expresses dissatisfaction with the present position.

20 Scratching is the effort of life to remove the dissatisfaction of the itch—as is urinating, defecating, sleeping, walking, working, playing, mating, talking, and moving about in general are all unsatisfied needs of life pushing man/woman always in the direction of more overall life satisfaction.

21 It is easy, in many cases, to recognize things that will satisfy us, such as obtaining money when funds are low, but it is extremely difficult at other times to comprehend the innumerable subconscious factors often responsible for the malaise of dissatisfaction.

22 Your desire to take a bath arises from a feeling of unseemliness or a wish to be refreshed, which means that you are dissatisfied with the way you feel at the moment; and your desire to get out of the bathtub arises from a feeling of dissatisfaction with a position that has suddenly grown uncomfortable.

23 This simple demonstration proves conclusively that man's will is not free because the attempt to attain more overall life satisfaction is the only direction life can take, and it offers only one possibility at each moment in time.

24 If you are depressed, anxious or angry in this current moment, then why not just use your "free will" and become less depressed, less anxious, or less angry?

25 You see, you cannot control these states. Hence, No Free Will. Believe it or not, you are sub/unconsciously attempting to gain more life satisfaction by being depressed, anxious, or angry.

26 These so-called negative states are in actuality the most satisfactory states you can be in at the current moment (presently available to you). They are in effect the lesser of two evils because you can always commit suicide (a greater evil).

27 I know you may feel that the negative states of anxiety, anger, and depression are not satisfying and therefore break the psychological and natural law that life can only take one direction and that is the direction of more satisfaction. Even though we feel anxiety, anger, and depression are not satisfying, they must be more satisfying by natural law than not being depressed, anxious, or angry on some deep-down level (sub/unconscious).

28 Negative feelings like anger, depression and anxiety exist. Hence, No Free Will.
29 Thoughts, feelings, and emotions come from background causes of which we exert no conscious control over. We cannot control the origin of our thoughts, feelings, and emotions. They come from background causes of which we are thoroughly unaware. You were not, are not, and will not be, in conscious control of your behavior which mandates that you must always seek out the most available life satisfaction.
30 You may not be able to predict what brings you the most life satisfaction available to you at any given time but that is not the point. The point is you are not in control of trying to attain the most satisfaction available to you at any given moment in time. You have no choice but to always be attempting to predict what will bring you the most amount of overall life satisfaction (available to you at the time) and act on that prediction. The fact that human beings are lousy at predicting what will give them the most overall life satisfaction is clearly beside the point.
31 Even though you never (or hardly ever) do something "against your will" that does not give you free will. This is a common mistake people make. People believe they have free will because they choose their preferences.
32 Everything you do is a lesser of two evils (or the least of many evils). You simply pick or choose the best possible option which you predict will give you the most amount of life satisfaction available to you at the time (from the viable options). This then becomes by default what you want to do (you have now chosen your preference/desire).
33 Choice is determined (caused) by desire. You choose your desire and then do what you desire to do (from a list of possibilities). This is why man rarely if ever does anything "against his will." The only real way to do anything against one's will is to be tied up and brought somewhere (or left in a place tied up) or forced to do or say something with a proverbial "gun to one's head." In other words, made or coerced to do or say something otherwise face death, bodily harm, loss of money, or some other negative consequence.

34 So even though man rarely if ever does something "against his will (desire)" this does not mean man's will is free. Hence, the confusion.
35 The truth is man cannot choose what he prefers. Preferences come from background causes for which man is completely unaware, exerts no conscious control of, and was not the originator of.
36 If I had a free will this new kind of Holy Bible would have been perfectly written and not been so repetitive. Thanks for reading.

The Holy Bible: No Free Will. Amen.

QUICK BOOK SUMMARY IS HERE

1. If Determinism is true, then there is no free will.
2. *If Indeterminism is true, then there is no free will.
3. Either determinism is true or indeterminism is true or some combination of both is true.
4. Therefore, there is no free will (from 1-3).

Quick Summary Part Two

Free will is not needed to keep society safe. It all depends on what level of the word "blame" we are discussing. There is the pragmatic and superficial level of the word "blame" (which keeps society safe) and the deeper, truer, and the fundamental level of the word "blame" (which means there is no heaven or hell).

Quick Summary Part Three

We have no choice but to seek pleasure and try to avoid pain. However, during our seeking we often have no choice but to experience unpleasant emotions which we have no control over. These unpleasant emotions then become part of our personal causal history and recondition us. There is no escape from this natural law of having no choice but to seek more and more overall life satisfaction. Everything is predetermined as we are always doing the very best we can with the data we had at the time.

---

* For the record I do not believe in indeterminism. Quantum mechanics is completely causal. Probabilities arise from underlying causality.

Law and Order will not break down with the advent of the knowledge contained in this book.

Actions will always still have *pragmatic consequences.

*see bottom of page 75

Many things we accept today as fact were ridiculed and opposed to in the not so distant past; this goes to show that just because an idea is currently unpopular does not mean it won't be unilaterally accepted in the future.

Please pass this book to another person if you understand why showing the world that free will doesn't exist will be the biggest thing ever to evolve the consciousness of our species.

If you for some reason cannot appreciate the importance of this work, then I will not blame you for your will is not free.

THOU SHALL NOT

FUNDAMENTALLY

BLAME

The Holy Bible: No Free Will. Amen.

www.ingramcontent.com/pod-product-compliance
Lightning Source LLC
LaVergne TN
LVHW091047100526
838202LV00077B/3072